MINDSET FOR BUSINESS

The Art and Science of Sound Decisions

Jane Turner

Published with the assistance of the Power Writers Publishing Group in 2021.

Jane Turner 2021.

All Rights Reserved. No part of this book may be reproduced by any mechanical, photographic, or electronic processes, or in the form of a phonographic recording. Nor may be stored in a retrieval system, transmitted or otherwise be copied for public or private use other than for 'fair use' - as brief quotations embodied in articles and reviews, without prior written permission of the publisher.

 A catalogue record for this book is available from the National Library of Australia

ISBN 978-0-6484230-5-8

Disclaimer

Any opinions expressed in this work are exclusively those of the author and are not necessarily the views held or endorsed by others quoted throughout. All of the information, exercises and concepts contained within the publication are intended for general information only. The author does not take any responsibility for any choices that any individual or organization may make with this information in the business, personal, financial, familial or other areas of life. If any individual or organization does wish to implement the ideas discussed herein, it is recommended that they obtain their own independent advice specific to their circumstances.

This book is available in print, and ebook formats.

DEDICATION

I honour you the reader

This book is dedicated to all the brave souls who have answered the call to start a business. And to all of those who haven't done that yet - but who desperately want to.

My deep gratitude goes to Carol Dweck, Tim Urban, Brene Brown and Joseph Campbell. Each of them wrote a book that changed my life.

Even deeper gratitude goes to Angela Vithulkas who works tirelessly to support businesses in Australia where I am based.

CONTENTS

Preface		i
Introduction		1
Chapter 1:	**Why Mindset Matters**	**15**
	Fixed vs Growth Mindset	15
	People Pleasing	18
	Negative Beliefs	22
	Secondary Gains	27
	Imposter Syndrome	29
	Core Beliefs Finder	32
Chapter 2:	**Neuroplasticity**	**33**
Chapter 3:	**Excuses Excuses**	**37**
	Perfectionism	39
	Procrastination	45
	Mindset Snapshot	48
Chapter 4:	**Developing a Success Mindset**	**51**
	Goal Setting	53
	Basic Goal Setting Exercise	55
Chapter 5:	**The Mind/Body Interface**	**57**
	Mind Decluttering Exercise	65
	Four Daily Rituals	70
	Three Grounding Minutes	71
	Three Focussed Minutes	72
	Three Relaxing Minutes	73
	Daylong Mindfulness	74
Chapter 6:	**The Hero's Journey**	**75**
	Hero's Journey Exercise	81
Chapter 7:	**The Author's Journey**	**85**
Chapter 8:	**Choice**	**93**
Conclusion		97
References		99
Resources		101
About The Author		103

PREFACE

I started writing this book on the fifth anniversary of the launch of my business.

Five years is a mere drop in the ocean when I compare it to the thirty-five plus years I spent working for the Australian government. In fact, the truth of it is that I spent my whole working life up to the age of fifty-two employed in a bureaucratic bubble, only to be made redundant and discover I was more or less clueless when it came to finding my way around the world of business.

It's been a steep learning curve for me, and I'm here to tell you that no matter where you are on the spectrum from clueless to clued-up on the business side of things, skilling yourself up on an emotional and psychological level is not something you want to neglect.

This is not a book written by someone with qualifications in any particular aspect of business. In fact, I still consider myself to have a long way to go in some regards. What I know for sure though, is that the mind is an incredibly valuable, and at the same time tricky facility to get the most out of. And knowing how to do that makes the world of difference.

PREFACE

My hope is that you will have a much better handle on how to make the most of the grey matter in your head after reading this book. Among other things, that will give you a much better chance of being able to make great decisions.

I've made my fair share of mistakes in terms of trusting untrustworthy people. Needless to say, back in the day I lacked a firm grounding to make decisions on. While I've been known to bitch about the 'snake oil salesmen' I've crossed paths with, one of the things I've loved most about being in business is the wonderful people I've been blessed to meet and collaborate with. Some of them have generously augmented what I've been able to provide from my own expertise. These people are experts in sales, financial management, communication skills and marketing. You'll find links to access these people in the appendix section.

I have to say I felt really proud as I read over everything for the last time prior to sending this book off to be printed. It gave me pause to reflect on what a beautiful thing it is to feel pride without self-doubt getting in the way of the sense of achievement I rightly deserve. You'll know why that's such a big deal for me soon. Suffice to say, that I was brought up in a place and time where parents were apt to say things like: "Don't big-note yourself," "Don't have tickets on yourself" and "Don't be a show pony."

INTRODUCTION

Right up to the end of the first quarter of 2020, when the impacts of the Covid-19 pandemic were being felt in Australia where I'm based, I was going to start this introduction by saying:

I have good news and I have bad news. The good news is that it has never been easier for entrepreneurs and small businesspeople to spread the word about their services.
The bad news is that it has never been easier for our competitors either.

The other piece of bad news is that the situation with Covid has made it even more important to do what you need to do to stay competitive, because with people being forced out of work at rates not seen since the Great Depression, consumer confidence is at an all-time low. One of the reasons for this is that uncertainty is at an all-time high, and people are more resistant than ever to spending money on things that they don't see as necessities.

I often hear people say things like "I don't feel confident doing …….. because I can't get a handle on what the world is going to look like in twelve months time." In fact, that's fair enough. But what most people don't recognise is that things can change

INTRODUCTION

dramatically in a heartbeat, with or without Covid. It's just that it used to be easier to believe this wasn't the case before we had direct experience of what it's like to have the rug pulled out from under us with markets drying up, the value of currencies going down, and 'freedoms' being curtailed all over the place.

Uncertainty is a particularly uncomfortable state for human being. While there are any number of good reasons to focus on developing a winning mindset, one of the best is to be able to be comfortable with uncertainty and the other states that make up the acronym VUCA (Volatility, Uncertainty, Complexity and Ambiguity).

I smile when I think about how I came across the idea of VUCA. It happened when I started working with a change management specialist who wanted to write a book to build her profile. Not surprisingly, she talks a lot about VUCA in the book she's writing at the moment. I smile because one of the things I love about what I do for work these days is that I'm continually learning and growing in the process. In fact, over the last twelve months I've worked with people who are writing books on laughter therapy, conscious ageing, succession planning, workplace relations, parity issues for women, branding, confidence, fitness, futurism, psychotherapy, the status of good men in the age of the #MeToo movement, and much more.

But enough about me. This book is all about you. It's about skilling you up to take your place in the 20 per cent of businesses that survive beyond the first five years. To do that, you need to be resilient, self-aware, doggedly determined and savvy enough to be able to sniff out a phoney at a thousand paces.

The last part of the sentence you just read alludes to the other piece of bad news I have for you. That is, that the sea of services available to people in the start-up phase, as well as those who are already in business and looking to level-up their results, are not always as they seem. God knows I've spent good money after bad on programs that were worth much less than I paid for them. In fact, a business coach I used to worked with once said that there are both sharks and dolphins in the ocean that service-based businesses like mine are operating within. And boy was she right.

That's actually one of the reasons I've written this book. I want you to be able to spot a shark from a mile off. In other words, I want to save you the trouble and expense of finding out first-hand what it feels like to be fleeced by a slick salesperson who is very good at winning your trust, and very slippery when it comes to fulfilling the promises they make, especially when it comes to the so-called 100 per cent satisfaction guarantee so many of these people lure their potential clients over the line with.

I figure if you're reading this book, you might have found out about sharks and dolphins yourself. Or if not, you're doing your due diligence before taking the leap from paid employment to running your own business. In either case, I want to congratulate you. You're in the right place to skill yourself up to make great decisions that will position you to get to where you want to be with the minimum of white noise, and wasted time and money.

The fact is, even if you're feeling totally unprepared and lacking in confidence right now, you will be in a much better position to succeed if you set yourself up with a mindset that supports you.

I share my story with you in the following pages because a few years ago I was in a place that probably looks a lot like where you are now. I'm living proof that it's worth putting the effort in to establishing a mindset that allows you to get out of your

INTRODUCTION

comfort zone, so that you can successfully make the transition from employee to business owner, or from being a business owner who is working way too hard for way too little, into one who is generating the results they need to feel satisfied and secure.

This question of comfort zones is important, because if you're looking to start a business or ramp up an existing one, your comfort zone is where that dream is likely to languish for a while, and then probably die. The sobering statistics around the rates of success and failure of businesses within the first five years are well known. My contention is that the fact that 80 per cent of small businesses eventually fail is an endorsement of the need to put the energy in to doing the mindset work. I say that because having a clear mind is critical to making sound decisions. Without it, the chance of winding up in the graveyard of failed businesses is just way too high.

My aim here is to either get you out of your comfort zone, or to stretch your comfort zone out to the point where it can encompass all of your goals. That includes setting up your business in a way that will not only be sustainable, but also highly profitable. That said, this is not a book about how to run a business per se. It's a book about getting your head in the game so that you don't unwittingly run interference on yourself.

I'm going to ask you a question that's likely to take you out of your comfort zone right now. That question is: "Why aren't you as successful as you would like to be?"

Are you telling yourself a story about not having the DNA of a businessperson, so getting past the six-figure threshold (or whatever yours is) is not something you could imagine doing in your wildest dreams? Or are you telling yourself that you couldn't stand the level of risk involved in transitioning from being an employee to being a business owner? Or is the story you're telling yourself related to the fact that the situation with Covid-19 has put the economy in such terrible shape that it's just too risky to start a business now?

There's no question that you have to tread carefully and get sound advice if you're contemplating leaving stable employment to start a business, or if you're floundering in a business that is taking in water and you don't know why. If your business (or the one you're thinking about starting) just doesn't have legs, then you might need to make some really tough decisions. Let's face it, if you take a long hard look at what's going on and realise that you've been limping along with shoddy systems, inadequate cash flow, lack of accountability, and too few customers to keep the business afloat, then a decent business coach could help you to set things straight. It could be that you just need to do the work to address your shoddy systems or whatever, or it might be about coming to terms with the fact that maybe your heart just isn't in it anymore. Whatever the case is, I'm glad you've found your way to this book.

I might not have all of the answers, but I'm confident that you will come out the other end of reading the chapters that follow with two important things. The first one is a reality check, and the second one is a set of strategies that will put you on the straight and narrow with a powerful mindset to move forward. With these two things on your side, you will have a solid foundation to make better decisions around questions like whether you need to change your processes, your prices, your messaging, or everything. And whether you need to call in professional help, or close-up shop altogether because keeping the business running is no longer a sustainable proposition.

INTRODUCTION

The bottom line is that maintaining a mindset that supports you to hit your goals will mean the difference between launching or scaling your business successfully, or forever craving the rewards that come with the so-called laptop lifestyle (or whatever your idea of that is). I know what it's like to sit in a state of craving. In fact, bringing the first book I wrote to launch my coaching business to life was a five-year journey with more twists and turns than a game of Snakes and Ladders. What came out the other end is a book called *Thrive in Midlife*. This is not a book that should have taken five years to write. It was never going to rub shoulders with *War and Peace* or *Anna Karenina*. These are the kinds of books you'd expect to be five or so years in the making. Mine, on the other hand, is a 30,000-word 'how-to' book that was written to build my authority and credibility as a coach.

These days I can write a book like this in a matter of a couple of months rather than years. I can do this by applying what I learnt over the course of my five-year odyssey. The learning curve I was on was especially steep just after a watershed moment at the end of 2014 when I was made redundant. I'd worked my way up to a healthy six figure salary after spending my whole working life (up to the age of fifty-two) employed by the Australian government. That moment when redundancy pulled the rug out from under me gave me the clarity I needed to be able to identify all of the barriers that were holding me back. Once I could identify them, I was able to work out what I needed to do to overcome them.

Working out how to align my mindset with the goal of getting my first book finished wasn't the only thing I identified at that time, but without a doubt it was the main piece of the puzzle I needed to have in place to make sure that the five years I'd already spent, didn't turn into six, seven, eight or more. Thinking back on the single most frustrating period of my life between 2009 and 2015,

I can now see that what kept me pushing on was the feeling I got in the pit of my stomach when I saw my competitors who had written books being handed opportunities that I was missing out on. Basically, I was being left behind, and I didn't like it.

Without knowing it, I was doing a lot more than just writing a book during those five long years. I was actually on a journey of self-discovery. In fact, it was a hero's journey. And the benefits of overcoming the barriers to getting my book written opened up my capacity to do some truly amazing things. Below, you'll find a summary of the decision points that got me to where I am now.

I've included this so you can start to think about how the kinds of roadblocks I experienced might be playing out in your own case.
- In 2009 when I was gainfully employed with a regular salary, I started to write a book on ageing well, but I soon got totally overwhelmed and filled with self-doubt. This led me to -
- Buy an online program that was marketed as having all of the templates and tutorials I would need to get my book finished, but –
- I soon hit a wall because the little voice in my head convinced me I was not qualified enough to promote myself as an expert through a book. So –
- I enrolled in a two-year transformational coaching course in 2010 which introduced me to the hero's journey.
  Note: Understanding the hero's journey motivated me to get back to writing. However, after a short period of renewed productivity, I settled back into another phase of mindset-related interference in the form of confusion, overwhelm and massive doses of procrastination.
- In 2014 I enrolled in one-on-one mentoring and a high-end writing retreat to finally get my book written. But -

- I soon hit another wall, and had to sit in the discomfort of the knowledge that -
  - I had invested over $30,000 in various writing courses and five years of my life in an attempt to become a published author.
  - I'd recently been made redundant from the job that had kept my family's finances afloat while I tried to write my book to grow my coaching business on the side.
  - I still didn't have a finished book to use to leverage the power of being a published author to raise my profile and grow my coaching business to the point where it could replace the six-figure salary I lost when I was made redundant.

  Note: This was a watershed moment that changed my life forever, because after sitting in the discomfort of the ugly truth of my situation for a while, I finally had a breakthrough and worked out what I needed to have in place to actually get my book finished.
- In 2015 I launched my first book *Thrive in Midlife* and developed *The Power Writing Program* to save my clients the kind of time and expense I went through to become a published author myself.
- I cracked the code to leveraging published author status to get free publicity. This led to the development of *The Power Publicity Program* in 2016.
- In 2017 I went on to write my second book in the 'Midlife' series, *Weight Loss in Midlife*, as well as launching an international speaking career by speaking at the Women's Economic Forum in India.
- In 2018 I wrote my third book, *Mindset for Authors: How to Overcome Perfectionism, Procrastination and Self-doubt,* and set up the *Power Writers Publishing Group* to offer a cost-effective option for my clients to get their books out into the world.

- At the end of 2018 I entered into an arrangement that taught me a lot about what **not** to do in business.
- In 2019 I got myself out of the business arrangement I mentioned above, launched my 'Author Showcase' events at the State Library of NSW, and put several of my female authors onto international stages through my affiliation with the Women's Economic Forum.
- At the end of 2019 I signed up with a business coach who helped me to get the business side of my business well and truly in order.
- In 2020 I set up a group coaching option within my *Power Writing and Business Development Program* to suit the specific circumstances presented by the Covid-19 situation, and I saw *Mindset for Authors* achieve International Best Seller status.
- In 2021 I set up The *Author Business Hub* to help my authors leverage their books to build their business.

I will always love my first book, even though I often joke about having written the wrong book. I say that because I never did get around to setting up a coaching practice to help women traverse the midlife phase (which is what I envisaged doing when I wrote *Thrive in Midlife*). Nevertheless, writing that book is what I had to do to become the person I needed to be to break out of the old patterns that positioned me to succeed within a bureaucracy. Those patterns had to be broken because they did not position me well to be successful in business. In fact I learnt a lot about myself in the process of writing that book, and the catharsis I experienced when I was on stage launching it. That catharsis took the shape of a blinding moment of clarity where I got to see that I was not put on this earth to help women through midlife. I was put on this earth to help people like me to share their story and their expertise, and tap into the Halo Effect of published author status.

INTRODUCTION

The great thing is that everything I learnt about mindset in the process of getting *Thrive in Midlife* finished, was equally applicable to building my business. That said, there was still a heck of a lot more learning I needed to do to overcome the challenges I faced once I launched my book. These challenges had to do with a number of things including:
- my relationship with money
- my negative beliefs around selling
- my need to avoid the snake oil salesmen who tell you that all you need is their insanely overpriced program to get to seven figures.

I'm blown away when I think about how many neural pathways I must have developed since 2014 when redundancy forced me to get real about what I was made of. I often say that writing a book is one of the best personal development courses you could ever do. As I think about it now, the same could be said about building a business.

With that in mind, I want you to picture me smacking my forehead with the palm of my hand in 2018 when I found that after all of the personal and professional development work I'd done over the previous decade, I was still able to be taken advantage of by a fast-talking operator who knew how to press all my buttons. I was like a lamb to the slaughter when this person managed to bypass the gatekeeper in my mind that was usually able to stop me from making dumb decisions. The cold, hard truth of it was that there was still a 'neediness' in me. That's what rendered me vulnerable to being taken for a ride. The situation at the time was that on the surface my business looked like it was going great guns, but in reality I was working way too hard for way too little. I had no solid systems in place, my pricing structure was out of whack, and I was a chronic people pleaser. So when someone who looked like he had all of the answers came onto the scene, I was easy prey because my head still wasn't totally in the game.

Not having my head totally in the game meant that I was able to believe that the knowledge and experience I had in the book-writing space, coupled with the fact that I was genuinely committed to helping my clients get the results they wanted, would be enough to get me over the line when it came to turning enquiries into sales. I'm not saying that these aren't important boxes for potential clients to be able to tick when they are sizing someone like me up, but what I am saying is that a lack of confidence and comfort around any aspect of what we do (especially if it relates to talking about the cost of the programs or services we offer), will outweigh whatever good standing our credentials broker for us with potential clients.

What I'm getting at here is that as recently as 2019 I had some clearly counterproductive and downright destructive mindset imprints playing out in my business. Fortunately, I found someone to help me to evolve beyond these, because having them in place was positioning me to be included in the 80 per cent of businesses that eventually fail.

I'm truly grateful to be able to say that I had completely turned things around by the end of 2019. These days I absolutely love the work I do in saving people from their version of my five years and over $30,000 worth of investment in writing programs that aren't really fit for purpose. But perhaps most satisfying of all is my ability to save my authors the heartbreak and potential financial disaster that can result from a wobbly business model and a mindset that is not totally honed-in on success.

You see, right from the get-go I was great at helping people write books to build their credibility and profile. And I was great at

INTRODUCTION

publishing books that perfectly represented my clients' personal and professional brands. What's more, I could show my authors how to promote their books like nobody else I know. But the elephant in the room was that I was terrible at business. So I took on a business coach at a diabolically low point in my journey where I had to sell the family home of 23 years because my business hadn't taken off as fast as I thought it would.

I know that to some people (including my husband), spending money on a coach was a crazy thing to do. I'd already tackled the problems I had with self-worth, and I had an unwavering belief in the value of what I had to offer, but I could see that if I was ever going to be able to bring enough money in to my business to justify keeping it running, I needed to get help to fast-track my learning around whatever I hadn't already worked out for myself.

I feel immense gratitude when I think back on the all-too-short time I spent working with Jane Copeland. She was the coach who got me up and out of the doldrums at the end of 2019. Among other things, Jane got me to see that I was doing the equivalent of trying to catch fish in a dry river, because I was spending good money and time on Facebook, while the kinds of clients my services really resonate with spend most of their time on LinkedIn. These two platforms are by no means mutually exclusive, but things really started to change dramatically for me when I cleaned up my LinkedIn profile, and concentrated a much higher proportion of my efforts there.

I mention this because I see too many people who resist getting help, and wind up either crashing and burning or stagnating, when they could be taking their success to a whole other level with solid advice from some of the great business coaches who are out there. Investing in coaching is something I highly recommend, because frankly, it is the only thing that stopped my business from going under.

I can't say I never have difficult days now. But what I can say is that you couldn't pay me to go back to the security of the 9-to-5. This is because I get an incredible buzz out of seeing people go from a place where they're focused on what they can't do, to a place where they categorically know in their heart and in their mind that they can write a book that will position them as an expert in their field.

CHAPTER 1: WHY MINDSET MATTERS

If we own our story, we get to write the ending.
If we don't, it owns us.
Brene Brown

This chapter is all about looking at the difference having a growth mindset rather than a fixed mindset will make to your ability to achieve your goals. I've focused on this to provide you with the skills you'll need to overcome the most common internal barriers that many people in the start-up phase in particular are likely to experience. The barriers I'm referring to here include things like perfectionism, procrastination, and self-doubt, as well as tendencies toward blame, justification and denial. The way I see it, being human involves experiencing these things, and being successful involves managing them.

FIXED vs GROWTH MINDSETS

A fundamental point you need to accept is that your ability to take responsibility for your outcomes is key. This is not an easy proposition for many people to take onboard. As Carol Dweck writes in her book, *Mindset: The New Psychology of Success,* there are essentially two overarching paradigms that help us to make sense of the way we interact with the world we live in. These paradigms are known as fixed and growth mindsets. This is important because our ability to come to terms with the question of personal responsibility is determined by where we sit on the continuum from a fixed to a growth mindset. The simple truth is that you will be relying on unreliable things, like dumb luck and extreme goodwill, if you don't hold yourself fully accountable for doing the work involved in achieving your goals.

People who primarily operate from a fixed mindset believe they are born with talents in some areas and not others. What's more, they believe this determines what they can and cannot achieve in life. You might hear someone with a fixed mindset say something like: "I'm highly creative, so I would never be any good at business." Or "I could never write a book, I'm just no good with words." Most of my clients are people with at least enough of a growth mindset to have thought something like: "I know I'm going to struggle with getting a book written because writing is not really my thing, so I'm going to enlist some help to make sure the project of writing my book doesn't sit on my bucket list forever."

Thinking about the difference between fixed and growth mindsets reminds me of something my father said when I was just a little kid. I can't remember exactly how old I was, but I know I wasn't in double digits when he said words to the effect that "You can't do anything about the cards you're dealt, but it's up to you to decide which cards you play." This kind of worldview implies opportunities to grow, as well as responsibility for taking the steps needed to allow growth to happen. That could mean signing up with a business coach, taking a writing course, hiring a personal trainer, or going back to university to retrain for a new career that requires specific qualifications.

Some people are more or less textbook cases of fixed mindset thinking, but most of us are more fluid than that. What that means is we approach some areas of life from a fixed mindset, and others from a growth mindset. We're even likely to approach certain areas of life from a fixed mindset some of the time, and from a growth mindset at others.

So let me ask you this: which mindset are you using to look at the question of how successful you can be? Are you buzzing with excitement about getting your message out into the world and feeling great about helping your clients get fantastic results? Or are you being stymied by limiting beliefs that stop you from setting your business up in a way that will enable you to live your life in a deeply satisfying way, whether that means being able to send your kids to a private school, or being able to build an orphanage in India, or being able to buy your own tropical island?

If the sentence about 'limiting beliefs' resonates with you more than the sentence about 'brimming with excitement', then you are part of the majority of people whose businesses are vulnerable to failure (if they ever get off the ground in the first place). In fact, if you resonated with the idea of brimming with excitement, then you probably wouldn't be reading this book in the first place. I say that because you'd be busy running your successful business already. But, as you are reading this book, I want you to know that no matter how your limiting beliefs might be manifesting right now, you will be able to shift things if you really take what I'm about to say on board. That is, that what's likely to be stymieing you a lot of the time is an unconscious need to avoid one of the most uncomfortable of all human states – vulnerability.

Avoiding vulnerability used to be my modus operandi. Needless to say, I had to learn to be comfortable with discomfort in order to do some of the amazing things I've done since becoming an author. These things include speaking on an international stage, appearing on television and in the press, and not only surviving but thriving within the dog-eat-dog world of the professional services market. Being able to do these things entailed breaking out of the safe and very contained mental space I had lived most of my life in. And that entailed coming to terms with the extent to which the insidious thing called Impostor Syndrome was sitting in the unconscious part of my mind. I've had to do some serious inner work to get to a place where I no longer feel vulnerable about being seen for who I really am. That was a big piece of the puzzle I needed to have in place to get my first book finished, and to get my introverted-self out to networking events and the like.

But that wasn't the end of the lessons I had to learn about the consequences of having a mindset that can trip us up from time to time, in spite of the ongoing investment we make in maintaining a growth mindset. In fact, it was much later in the piece when I got comfortable with having conversations around money in general, and about talking to clients who had fallen behind in their payment plans in particular. Working on my money mindset and my people-pleasing tendencies enabled me to see that one of the things making me uncomfortable in this territory was a displaced need to be loved. It was this need that caused me to suffer from many of the classic problems that people pleasers deal with on a day-to-day basis.

PEOPLE PLEASING

According to Sherry Pagoto who is a clinical psychologist and Associate Professor of Medicine at the University of Massachusetts, "people pleasing is either driven by a fear of rejection and/or a fear of failure." Fear of rejection often develops out of early childhood experiences that undermine our self-esteem. From an evolutionary standpoint, being shunned or rejected by the extended family group that we rely on for survival could result in death. So even though having a neglectful, or even absent parent isn't necessarily a life-threatening situation these days, we are physiologically and psychologically wired in such a way that our response to rejection is exactly the same as it was back in the day when being accepted was literally a matter of life or death.

The companion to fear of rejection is fear of failure. Fear of failure is embedded in the belief that making a mistake will result in our looking stupid, and/or getting into trouble, which in turn will result in being rejected in one way or another. It's the double-whammy of fear of rejection and fear of failure that bears down on a lot more people than you might imagine. Believe me – it's not just you.

Fear of failure is most likely to develop out of experiencing harsh criticism, ridicule and/or punishment when we're young. This can lead to experiencing anxiety and/or fear when it comes to taking on new and challenging tasks as adults. This plays out in people doing whatever it takes to avoid or mitigate the anxiety. In most cases, that means not taking on the challenging task in the first place. But if we can't avoid taking it on, then we will put in an extraordinary amount of effort to make sure we do the job perfectly.

In addition to this section on people pleasing, you will find sections on things like perfectionism and negative beliefs as you move through the chapters that follow. All of these things are linked to the root cause, which is the avoidance of vulnerability.

Don't get me wrong on the question of people pleasing. Wanting to do the right thing by people is not a bad thing per se. It's only when you do it to the exclusion of your own needs that it becomes a problem. As the author of *Risky is the New Safe*, Randy Gage says:

Living a life of self-sacrifice enables others to take advantage of you, and when practised long enough it will ultimately destroy you if you have no other purpose in life than placating others and seeking approval which you can only earn by giving up your own happiness.

Paradoxically, people pleasing is not only a bad deal for the people pleaser, but it also backfires on the people they are trying to help as well. This is because the exhaustion and frustration that goes hand-in-hand with being a chronic people pleaser drains the energy we need to be able to operate at our very best, and thus deliver excellent service to our clients.

Sadly, extreme people pleasing tendencies played out in the early days of my business in a number of significant ways. One of them was my unwillingness to get out of my comfort zone and have difficult conversations with people who owed me money. Another was the ridiculous length of time it took me to speak up about not being provided with anywhere near the value I should have received out of a $37K investment in a business-building program I signed up for.

Importantly, I also had to come to terms with the fact that my programs weren't going to sell themselves. In fact, in the bad old days, I felt so icky about coming across as salesy in the regular half-day workshops I ran to recruit people into my writing programs, that I didn't even issue a call to action at the end of the event. I cringe when I think about how crazy it was to expect people to be so taken with my obvious know-how and genuine desire to help them become published authors, that they would run up to me and beg me to take them on as clients before they left the room. Of course, that didn't happen. And over time, as my bank balance shrunk, the idea that I had to do some serious work on my hang-ups around my relationship with money, and my identity as someone with something to sell, finally sunk in. Needless to say, failing to come to terms with things like these sooner rather than later cost me dearly in terms of forestalling the results I deserved to be achieving.

An unintended and essentially unconscious consequence of this was a kind of simmering resentment, verging on passive aggression towards some of my clients. This came about because I was silently angry at the people who had welched on my invoices and/or driven me down on the price of my programs. This hurt me both in terms of the income I was generating, and in terms of the quality of the relationships I had with the penny-pinching culprits who were in the early cohort who signed up to work with me. This was a real shame because what matters most to me is the quality of the relationships I have with my clients.

At the end of the day, what I had to do to purge myself of people pleasing tendencies was build my confidence and self-esteem. This entailed clearing out the baggage I'd developed over the course of my life. This baggage was contaminating my self-worth in general, and my beliefs around money in particular. I know there's still a little bit of the people pleaser in me. But these days I'm aware of it, and when I catch myself lapsing into old unhelpful habits, all I need to do is tap into my purpose. Being in that state ultimately serves my clients much better than people pleasing ever could.

The thing I had to do once I had a solid foundation to move forward with, was establish healthy boundaries in my business and in my life. I have to say that the empowerment I experienced once I got around to sticking up for myself, far outweighed any of the initial discomfort I might have caused my clients by reminding them of the ground rules I put in place to make their responsibilities clear to them upfront. In fact, developing a set of ground rules about what is and isn't included in the services I offer makes it so much easier to induct clients into my programs. I have my ex-coach Jane Copeland to thank for putting me on the straight and narrow in relation to establishing absolute clarity for my clients and myself about the boundaries in my business.

I'm incredibly grateful to be able to coach my clients who are using their book to launch a service-based business, to establish ground rules to induct their clients into their programs. It just saves so much time and potential for confusion. As Pagoto says:

We teach people how to treat us by the behavior we accept or reject from them. If someone takes advantage of you, it is only their fault once. After that it is your fault for not teaching them different.

Teaching them different in the context of running a service-based business includes setting boundaries about what you will and will not accept, and establishing clarity around what the client needs to do to achieve their goals vis-a-vis the services you are offering.

NEGATIVE BELIEFS

An important piece of the puzzle is that we all have a set of core beliefs that determine every decision we make. For most people, they are not all negative. However it's the negative beliefs we are interested in here because they underlie people pleasing and other counterproductive things like self-sabotage. The bottom line is that carrying around a stack of negative beliefs will undermine our ability to see ourselves as successful. And in that way, they will make it difficult to make decisions that align with our values and the goals we set for ourselves.

This kind of thing is not taught in schools. And unless you've done some personal development work or studied psychology or coaching (either formally or by way of the books you've read), you might not have ever thought about what your core beliefs are. In fact, you might not have even been aware that you had any. Let me explain. Core beliefs show up in the fundamental understanding we have about ourselves, other people, and the world we live in. They reside under our conscious thoughts and impact every decision we make. For example, our core beliefs determine whether we see ourselves as worthy, safe, competent, powerful, lovable and any number of other positive or negative states. One of my favourite quotes from Albert Einstein is, "The most important decision you will ever make, is whether you live in a hostile world or not."

One of the main problems with negative beliefs is that while they are unconscious, they are incredibly powerful and self-perpetuating. Another thing about them is that they can only exist because of the blinkers they force us to see the world through. For example, when you constantly tell yourself you are not good enough, you will only notice things that prove this belief to be true. That's because one of the fundamental states we strive for as human beings is congruity. So if we believe we are not good enough to be successful in business, we will unconsciously sabotage any results that would provide evidence to the contrary.

Core beliefs are the foundations of self-worth. They are behind our understanding of what we can and cannot do. In that way, they actually inform the 'rules' we live by. These rules play out on an unconscious level every single day of our life. Essentially, they are the guiding principles we make decisions on. So, while rules are not a problem per se, they become a problem when they limit us by stopping us from doing the things necessary to reach our goals.

Let's see how this might play out in the real world.

If we believe we are a failure for example, our rules could include things like:
- Never try hard at anything (because we'll only fail anyway).
- Never ask questions or challenge the opinions of others (because we'll probably be wrong and look foolish).
- Never expect to get ahead (because we don't have what it takes, and the disappointment of failure is too much to bear).
- Never apply for a promotion (because it will be embarrassing and soul destroying when we don't get it).
- Never quit a job (because we won't be able to get another one).

Breaking one of these rules by succeeding rather than failing has the potential to unsettle our equilibrium because it would be incongruent with our core beliefs. On the other hand, if the outcome is not incongruent and we do actually fail, then the experience will deliver another blow to our self-esteem because it will confirm that we are indeed 'a failure'.

Another example we can take a look at here is the belief that we are unworthy. In this case, our rules might include:
- Never ask for anything, especially help.
- Always work extra hard.
- Never say no in spite of the negative consequences of agreeing to do something we don't want to do.
- Strive to be perfect all of the time.
- Live in fear of making a mistake because the shame of it would be unbearable.

The truth is that most people unconsciously agree to live with the negative consequences their limiting beliefs force onto them. That's not the case for everyone though, and it definitely won't be the case for you if you commit to doing the exercises in this book and seek help if you feel like you need it. The people I work with have a goal to get from their present state to their desired state. And because they have a growth mindset, they know on a fundamental level that they can get there if they are prepared to get out of their comfort zone and follow the steps I set out for them.

The first and most important step in this scenario is to identify the desired state. Most of my clients are businesspeople who want to increase their visibility and credibility by becoming a published author. Therefore, their desired state is to have a book published that positions them as the go-to person in their field. But that desired state is a bit too general. So I ask my clients to imagine themselves twelve months down the track with a published book, and describe in detail what that will look like. Maybe they've put their coaching rates up. Maybe they're being paid for speaking at conferences and events (rather than struggling to even get unpaid speaking opportunities). Maybe they're able to afford to go on holidays, or something else they've been longing to do.

This is important because there's enormous power in having a clear representation of your outcome in mind. For instance, if you're like I was seven years ago – someone who had only ever been an employee with a clear set of tasks and a guaranteed income capped at whatever level it was capped at – then you need to be able to envisage a totally different life. You need to be able to get a vision of what life will look like in terms of what you'll be doing and feeling, and who you will be showing up as in your relationships and your business.

I'm covering the topic of beliefs before talking about goal setting because if your goals are incongruous with the beliefs you hold about who you are and what you can achieve, then self-sabotage is likely to get in the way. As I said earlier, this is because our unconscious mind cannot cope with incongruity, so we default to running interference on ourselves to maintain the status quo. Counterintuitively though, one of the ways to change our beliefs is to start acting 'as if' we already have the goal we are working towards.

Until I did Neuro Linguistic Programming (NLP) training as part of my coaching qualifications, I had no idea about any of this stuff. I was a university educated, middle class woman, who was hunkered down in stable employment within the bureaucracy of the Australian government for decades. But a crack appeared in the identity I wore like a coat of armour when I found out (through an NLP process called 'Time Line Therapy') that I was the surviving twin in a case of vanishing twin syndrome. Needless to say, this was a huge shock that really rattled me. In fact, it led to the gradual peeling back of the onion layers around all the limiting beliefs I had incorporated into my worldview over the fifty or so years I'd been alive.

I'm not sharing this information about my own case with you because you need to know the information itself. I'm sharing it to encourage you to start thinking about what might be going on in your own case that is undermining your confidence, and your ability to do the things you need to do to get to your dreams.

You'll find an exercise at the end of this chapter to drill down into the question of what your core beliefs are. One of the reasons I want you to get your head around this is because you might not realise you could actually be receiving some benefit from the problems you are trying to solve. What I'm referring to here is a phenomenon called secondary gains. In the world of coaching and psychology, secondary gains are the piece of the puzzle that makes sense of self-sabotage and other behaviours stopping people from taking the actions they need to take to achieve their goals.

SECONDARY GAINS

Secondary gains are the 'benefits' we get from NOT overcoming a problem that on the surface we are desperately trying to overcome. For many people who are stuck, the phenomenon of secondary gains helps makes sense of what's really going on.

Here are some hypothetical examples to help you understand how secondary gains work.

Example One
A person who is increasingly finding the pressure of their work overwhelming, happens to catch a mild flu. In spite of the fact that the strain of flu going around at the time is not particularly virulent, in this person's case it drags on for weeks that turn into months, and eventually their condition morphs into chronic fatigue syndrome. They are certainly not enjoying being unwell, and they are not doing anything to keep themselves that way, but the reality is that if they get 'unsick' they will have to return to work and subject themselves to the pressure they were experiencing before they went off on sick leave. Notwithstanding the fact that some people actually have compromised immune systems that make it harder for them to get well after an illness, secondary gains could be playing out in relation to this particular person because the positive side to being unwell is that they have a reason for not going back to work where they would be subjected to the feelings of stress and overwhelm they experienced previously.

CHAPTER 1: WHY MINDSET MATTERS

Example Two
A person is scared of succeeding almost as much as they are of failing. They know that making changes to their processes at work would give them a much better chance of being promoted, but they don't maintain the changes they start to make. This happens because as soon as they see their results improving, they get a spike in anxiety about succeeding. To avoid the anxiety, they sabotage their results by slackening off on the things that were starting to increase their productivity.

Example Three
A lonely person is putting their life on hold by never taking up opportunities to go out and socialise. They are turning down invitations to go out because the voice in their head tells them they need to lose ten kilos before anyone would be interested in them. What's going on here is the result of unresolved pain from an ugly breakup that took place a decade earlier. Focusing on losing weight, without ever actually doing anything about making it happen, is helping this person avoid the risk of having to feel the sting of rejection again by putting themself out there. No matter how many diets they go on, they will always fail because the discomfort around their weight is not nearly as anxiety provoking as the idea of opening up the old wound they sustained a decade earlier when they were dumped by somebody they were keen on.

All of this is happening at the level of their unconscious mind. I mention that because I want you to know that falling into the secondary gains trap is not a negative reflection on someone's character. It's a behavioural mechanism people get trapped in without even knowing it's happening. The person who developed chronic fatigue syndrome for example, was not faking it or purposely keeping themselves sick. They were tangled in a psychological trap that profoundly compromised their health in particular, and the quality of their life in general.

What I want you to know is that there is no need to worry if you recognise any secondary gains playing out in your own life. I say this because you can easily learn alternative coping strategies for getting your needs met.

What I'd like you to do now is pause for a moment to consider whether you have a persistent problem playing out in your own life at the moment. Once you've identified it, I want you to think about whether you are avoiding doing the kinds of things a reasonable person would do to solve or improve the problem. If you are, I want you to think about whether there are any 'benefits' that come along with staying stuck, rather than moving beyond the problem. Identifying this might be all it takes to break free of the particular secondary gains trap you're stuck in. It's not always that simple though. So if you feel like you need help with this, I want you to take action and get the help you need sooner rather than later.

IMPOSTOR SYNDROME

The mother of all manifestations of the belief that 'we are not good enough' is called Impostor Syndrome. Notwithstanding what I know about Impostor Syndrome from my own direct experience of it, I've also learnt an awful lot about it from the clients I work with in my book coaching practice. In fact, it breaks my heart to see incredibly competent and well-credentialed people being crippled by self-doubt and feelings of inadequacy. These people tend to be particularly risk averse. They go out of their way to over-perform for fear of 'being found out', and they're likely to shy away from any opportunities they feel challenged by.

Obviously, Impostor Syndrome sits within a fixed mindset. No matter how much evidence there is to the contrary, those who are afflicted with it are convinced they will be 'found out' for not being as smart and competent as everyone else thinks they are. And no matter how much positive feedback the world gives them to the contrary, they're simply not able to establish a realistic appreciation of their abilities.

I'm not saying everyone who either fails to put the work in to achieve their version of success, or who goes overboard and puts in twice as much effort as they need to, is afflicted with Impostor Syndrome. But I do want to suggest you take some time to reflect on exactly what it is that's stopping you from moving forward.

Unlike people operating from a fixed mindset, those who operate from a growth mindset approach challenges with a high degree of curiosity, and remain open to learning new things throughout their life. Sure, they might never make it to the Olympics or become a Rhodes Scholar, but they know they can improve their level of skill in anything they put their mind to. For people with a growth mindset, it's all about improvement – not perfection.

As Dweck explains, it comes down to the question of how we react to challenges. Do we give up when we're challenged because we can't bear the idea of failing, or we fear being shown up as not as good as everyone thinks we are? Or do we keep working away at challenges in the knowledge our failures are just stepping stones to growth?

The good news is that you can develop a growth mindset no matter where you are on the fixed to growth continuum. According to Dweck, developing a growth mindset starts with becoming aware of the language of the fixed mindset, and recognising that we ultimately have a choice when it comes to how we react to it. We need to deliberately engage the voice of our growth mindset to flip the narrative around whenever we hear the voice of our fixed mindset saying something like, "What's the point of even starting this book when you know you'll never get it finished anyway?" Then we need to go on and take the kind of action a person operating from a growth mindset would take. If we continue to be persistent in this regard, we will slowly but surely reprogram our brain, and change our life forever.

Dweck's strategy to move from a fixed mindset to a growth mindset is one of the most powerful tools I know of when it comes to establishing a supportive internal environment. That's the kind of environment we need to be able to kick things like self-doubt to the kerb. So I've laid the strategy out for you in a step-by-step format here.

Step One
Recognise fixed mindset thinking as it emerges.

Step Two
Refute it with growth mindset thinking.

Step Three
Take the kind of action a person with a growth mindset would take.

Step Four
Repeat Steps 1 to 3 as required.

CORE BELIEFS FINDER

What we're going to do now is a bit of digging to see what some of your core beliefs might be. This is an exercise I recommend you do at least yearly to keep your focus sharp. Whatever you do, don't skip over it now. You'll see that I've shaded all of the areas in this book where I want you to pause and delve into your own situation. Coming back and answering the questions later (or not answering them at all) will rob you of the opportunity to get the most out of the time you're investing in reading this book.

1. Bring a thought you often have about yourself to mind. An example might be: "I'm too sensitive to be a successful businessperson."
2. Ask yourself, "What does that mean about me?" An example might be: "I'm not tough enough" or "I'm scared I will fail."
3. Ask yourself again, "What does that mean about me?"
4. An example of a response might be: "I'm weak" or "I'm a failure." *** **"I'm a failure"** might be your core belief.
5. To test this out, you can ask yourself again, "What does that mean about me?"

If nothing comes up when you ask that question, then **"I'm a failure"** is your core belief.

Meanwhile something like **"I'm not good enough"** might come up. In that case **"I'm not good enough"** is your core belief.

The exact language your unconscious mind uses is what matters here. That's why we keep drilling down until we hit bedrock.

CHAPTER 2: NEUROPLASTICITY

*The mind that opens to a new idea never
returns to its original size.*
Albert Einstein

The beauty of being human is that we're infinitely flexible. We have Norman Doidge to thank for making the phenomenon called neuroplasticity accessible to the layperson through his great book, *The Brain That Changes Itself*. Neuroplasticity means we literally change the structure of our brain as we engage with the world around us. In other words, behaviours are not as hardwired as we might have been led to believe. This means our past only dictates our future to the extent we choose to capitulate and keep repeating old patterns. But if we're prepared to put the work in to first recognise, and then break the old patterns of thinking and behaving that no longer serve us, then we will tap into our innate ability to learn and grow from the time we are born to the time we die.

Children tend to naturally operate from a growth mindset. It's great to watch them exploring their world with immense curiosity and very little fear of failure. But most of us unlearn this approach to some degree as we move through our life in families, schools and workplaces that are more likely to reward us for what we achieve, rather than rewarding us for our attitude in general, and our tenacity to work through challenges in particular.

Dweck's research shows that those who are consistently rewarded for doing their best and persisting with tasks they are challenged by, not only go on to have strengths in relation to focus and perseverance, but also to develop skills like resilience and tenacity. These skills set them up to fare well when adversity strikes. Whereas those who are only praised for getting high grades and coming first aren't exposed to nearly as many opportunities to develop these critical coping skills. Worse still, they are likely to associate their worth with their achievements, in which case failure of any kind is an incredibly frightening prospect.

Given what I know now, I can distinctly remember what my fixed mindset was telling me during the period between 2009 (when I started to write my first book) and the end of 2014 (when I finally passed it on to my editor). The idea of writing a book came to me when I bumped into an old friend I hadn't seen for ages. The thing that struck me about her was that she looked at least a decade younger than she did when I saw her years earlier. It was as if she'd worked out how to turn back the clock. When she told me she was on a wellness program being run by the naturopath she was seeing, I jumped onto the naturopath's website to find out how I could sign up to get some of what my friend was having. But the wind went out of my sails when I noticed the naturopath's practice was a 90 minute drive from where I lived and worked. When I factored in the regular four hour round trip required every second week to sign up for the program my friend was on, I decided I'd have to be crazy to even think about it. But just as I was about to let go of the idea, I noticed the naturopath was the author of a book about how women approaching midlife could increase their chances of ageing well through nutrition. Suddenly, the idea of signing up with this naturopath didn't seem that crazy after all.

Once I found out about the naturopath's book, I assumed she was totally credible, and as far as I was concerned, she was the go-to person for women in midlife who wanted to feel good about themselves. In other words, her status as an author increased my sense of trust in her ability to broker the results I was looking for.

The phenomenon that brought my change of heart about is called the Halo Effect. The Halo Effect accounts for the fact that the naturopath's status as an author cancelled out the obvious inconvenience of having to take half a day off work every two weeks to work with her.

The Halo Effect explains the tendency we have to attribute qualities to people or things that aren't necessarily attributable to them. We see it at work in the world of advertising all the time. For example, we might not consciously think that drinking Coca-Cola will transform us into carefree, beautiful young things like the people we see in the advertisements. However, that's the connection we make at a subconscious level when we grab a six-pack on our way to a picnic or whatever. The Halo Effect also explains why celebrities are paid ridiculous amounts of money to endorse everything from cars to watches and coffee pods. It also explains why I was prepared to enter into an extremely inconvenient and costly arrangement with a naturopath who ran her business miles away from where I spent most of my time.

The story of my friend and her naturopath is a particularly potent one for me. It not only gave me a direct experience of the power of the Halo Effect, but it also gave me the idea of writing a book to pave my transition from wage-earner to business owner when the time was right for me to make the break from the security of a regular payslip.

CHAPTER 2: NEUROPLASTICITY

All of this was a big deal for me because I didn't just go through a transformation in terms of becoming an author when I wrote my first book. I also went through a transformation in terms of becoming someone who was more inclined to approach life from a growth mindset than a fixed mindset. The freedom and empowerment that came along with that change has helped me grow in almost every area of my life. Sometimes I have to pinch myself when I think about the incredible things I've done since overcoming the barriers to fully stepping into my story and getting my first book written. In fact, I would go so far as to say that I experienced a catharsis when I was writing *Thrive in Midlife*. That catharsis resulted in my becoming a much more focused and grounded person who backs herself 100 per cent whenever she sees an opportunity that's worth pursuing. There's nothing even remotely resembling Impostor Syndrome in my world anymore. And believe me, this is very different to the way things were prior to 2014.

These days, when I meet with potential clients who are contemplating signing up for my *Power Writing Program*, I explain that in addition to providing them with a number of strategies to align their mindset with the goal of completing their book, the program also includes a framework that makes it very clear where to start, and what steps to take to get over the finish line with a minimum of angst and confusion. Even so, I know that no matter how clear I've made the steps, it's likely that one or more disempowering states will kick in at some stage. This is where my background as a coach with fifteen years of experience in NLP really comes into its own. It's also why I developed a program for my clients that is tantamount to holding their hand through the whole process from idea, to writing, to publishing, to promoting and finally to building a business around their books.

CHAPTER 3: EXCUSES EXCUSES

He who is good at making excuses is seldom good at anything else.
Benjamin Franklin

The program I offered aspiring authors when I first launched my business was a fairly straightforward series of writing workshops. Over time, it developed into the complete offering I mentioned earlier, because I soon learnt that to make it really work, I had to be able to fully negate the plethora of creative excuses that come up when I ask my clients why they haven't started or finished their book yet. Asking this question in the way that I do often leads to the light going on for people who sign up with me to fast-track themselves to published author status. In particular, the importance of mindset really hits home when we start to tease out exactly how they've been taken out of the game by a mindset that defaults to making excuses. This is tantamount to saying it defaults to not taking responsibility.

The most common form excuses tend to take are blame, justification and denial. I've heard some great examples during the initial conversation I have with potential clients about how my

CHAPTER 3: EXCUSES EXCUSES

program could work for them. They often start off by saying they've wanted to write a book for ages, but haven't done it yet because …
- I'm not one of those people who is gifted with words, so I'm on the back- foot when it comes to writing a book.
- I've tried everything to write my book, but I just can't do it.
- It's my husband's fault. I can't be expected to pump out a book after a hard day at work, as well as keeping everything ticking over in the household.

Or some other version of what essentially amounts to the person not being ready to step up, take responsibility and fully back themself.

This kind of thinking keeps would-be authors stuck because it makes it possible for them to believe their lack of progress can be explained by something other than their failure to take responsibility for their outcomes. In the case of my first book, it just got way too hard for me to maintain this kind of thinking once I got wise about how illogical and disempowering the stories I'd concocted to avoid sitting down to write actually were.

I'm in a much better place now after working my way out of the tangled web I was stuck in for the best part of the five years it took me to write my first book. For me, the key to all of this was learning how to look for clues about what was really going on inside my head. Then I could either go on to heal whatever needed healing, or engage in some tough love and remind myself that I was responsible for enlisting the burden of choice that all human beings have. In other words, I had to break the patterns that had kept me stuck in so many areas of my life for so long.

As I mentioned earlier, it was only when my circumstances forced me to sit in the discomfort of having spent over $30,000 and five years of my life in an attempt to write my first book, that I was able to identify the excuses I'd been telling myself. Once I identified these, I was able to delve into the deep need they were distracting me from. That need turned out to be related to a profound sense of insecurity playing out as Impostor Syndrome. Essentially, I had to contend with immense fear and self-doubt that took the form of a bully inside my head. This bully continually told me that everyone would probably think my book was crap, and nobody would end up buying it anyway because I didn't have a platform to promote it from. At the same time, I was having to deal with a monumental struggle between the part of myself that knew I had to tell my whole story for the book to have the impact I wanted it to have, with the other part of myself that desperately wanted to keep silent about the existence of an eating disorder I'd held as a deep dark secret for decades.

The solution to all of this was to garner the resources I needed to be able to step up and face the bully in my head. That's what got me to the point where I could fully own the good, the bad and the ugly of who I truly was. That's what allowed me to finally let go of the veil of competency and functionality that my ego made sure I fronted up to the world wearing every single day of my life.

Needless to say, getting beyond these kinds of barriers can take some pretty intense work. And believe me, I know how tempting it is to turn a blind eye to what's going on under the surface. But I can put my hand on my heart and say with complete conviction, that knowing what I know now about the doors that open for businesspeople who really know their stuff, I would happily do the work ten times over to get to where I am now.

PERFECTIONISM

I know I'm probably killing a sacred cow when I treat perfectionism as an excuse, rather than elevating it to a phenomenon that sits out on its own, above all others. What I want to say about that, is while I don't mind acknowledging that perfectionism is not your run-of-the-mill excuse, there's no way I'm going to give it the kind of respect I see way too many people giving it. In fact, it really galls me when I see people wearing perfectionism as if it's some kind of badge of honour, especially if they use it to explain their lack of progress by glorifying the fact that they always hold themselves up to the highest of high standards. This kind of delusional thinking puts an all-but impenetrable barrier between perfectionists and their dreams. What I want you to see here is that perfectionism is just another strategy people like you and I use to avoid taking responsibility, thereby justifying not doing the work we need to do to get to our goals.

I see the impact of perfectionism in my coaching practice all the time. I'd go so far as to say it's one of the most common reasons people choke in the process of trying to get their books finished. And the same goes for my clients who are setting up webinars, or online programs, or membership sites. Perfectionism works by compelling us to do something perfectly or not doing it at all. This often results in any number of crazy things coming into play. A great example I often see is people who are writing content going over and over the same small chunk of text, tweaking it to within an inch of its life. In fact, I once had one of my book-writing clients ask me if a comma should be here or there, because he had been trying it in both places for about twenty minutes and couldn't work out where it should go. I can still see the shock on his face when I said, "I don't frigging care. Let the editor decide when the time comes." The technique I used is called a Pattern Interrupt. It's a tactic that shocks people into a state of heightened awareness and pushes them out of the train of thought that's keeping them trapped in a cycle of compulsively checking and tweaking their content until the cows come home. I use this technique because fixating about the position of a comma is not only a terrible waste of time, but it also puts people at risk of totally running out of energy and passion in the process of chasing that elusive 'perfect' sentence.

What I advise my book-writing clients to do from the outset is resist the urge to edit their material at all when they're working on their first draft. In fact, if you are writing a book, and you get nothing else out of reading this one, I want you to know you're much more likely to get over the finish line if you don't try to edit your text at all until you get all of the content out of your head and on to the page.

I not only advise my clients to hold off editing their work too early in the process, I also encourage them to avoid seeking advice from every Tom, Dick and Harry. I've seen authors led down the garden path by well-meaning friends who don't know anything about what matters to the target audience for the book. I'm not talking about giving your final draft to a 'qualified' beta reader before sending it off to be proofread, or asking for feedback from a writing coach with well-developed editing skills like me. What I'm talking about here is not leaving yourself open to having to do a whole lot more work on your book (or webinar, or keynote speech, or whatever) for very little or no gain in the end.

The other thing I encourage my authors to do is celebrate small wins along the way. What I call 'modest milestones' include things like finishing sections within chapters, or getting out of one's comfort zone and posting content on social media at least three times a week. It's really important to pause and celebrate these things because we need to recharge our engines before we get down to the job of rearranging the material within and across chapters. In the case of my clients who are writing books to build their profile and expert status, it's only after that initial chunk of work is done that it's safe to bring out their word-smithing and comma-positioning skills. Doing this too early in the process is tantamount to digging a big hole that the author-to-be might never get out of.

Perfectionism is given a chapter of its own in some books about mindset. That's how big of a deal it can be. But when I really thought about it with the perspective I have after coming out the other side as an author of four books (and counting), I realised what I wanted readers like you to take away from this chapter is the understanding that just as you are neither owned nor defined by a tendency to react to things with a fixed or a growth mindset, neither are you owned or defined by a history of responding to life's circumstances with a perfectionist mindset.

What all of this amounts to on a practical level is that the sooner you get comfortable with a clunky and possibly downright ugly first draft of your book (or whatever it is you're working on), the better. One of my clients recently told me he was struggling because he felt repulsed by his book. After we agreed on an accountability strategy that would keep him moving forward no matter how he was feeling about his book at any given time, I suggested he think back to the time when he made his first cake. I asked him to remember that all he needed to do was work to a proven recipe and be relaxed about whatever mess was involved, because he could be confident that the finished product would not carry any stains from the process that brought it about.

What I'm getting at here, is that even very experienced writers and businesspeople don't get to beat the rap on the messy part of the process of getting over the finishing line (whatever that might be). So if you're new to business and want to reap the rewards that are out there for those who get the business side of their business right, you need to get comfortable with the less than pretty setup phase. What's more, just as it's sensible for inexperienced cooks to use a recipe when they're learning to cook, it's also sensible for start-ups, or people whose businesses are floundering, to follow the advice of someone who's gone before them.

One of the biggest lessons I've learnt so far, is that trying to be everything to everyone is a bad move. So what I've done is bring a number of experts who complement my strengths into my team. My strengths relate to knowing how to help businesspeople write expert-positioning books. I'm not an expert when it comes to SEO. I'm not an expert in financial management. Nor am I an expert in workplace efficiency, or any number of other areas of business. I have these kinds of people around me if I need advice, and to refer my clients to when they need help outside of my area of expertise.

I look back and kick myself for not reaching out for help sooner than I did. I can only wonder at the amount of foregone revenue I left behind because of a lack of systems and structures that would have enabled me to capitalise on the opportunities out there for people with a clear message that is consistently delivered to the right audience.

I had a conversation with a wellness coach recently who told me that it felt extravagant to invest in herself and her book by engaging a coach and an editor. So I suggested she calculate the opportunity-cost she was absorbing when she left money on the table by forestalling the business growth that would open up when she was able to leverage the credibility and authority of being a published author of a book was both readable and marketable. As sensible as this advice may sound, sadly the reality is that the world is littered with would-be authors and floundering businesspeople who compromise their ability to get their message and services out there, because they are not willing to spend money on the help they need.

I'm emphasising the importance of aligning your mindset with your goals here because I know the difference it will make. In my own case, I was totally at the mercy of my mind running its default programs before I got a handle on the question of mindset. One of those default programs involves what Eckhart Tolle calls "compulsive, involuntary thinking." This is a classic energy-sapper and potentially a spirit-breaker too. While many of the thoughts we have are benign enough, sooner rather than later businesspeople (especially in the start-up phase) are going to have to deal with automatic negative thoughts that seem to spring up out of nowhere. They're the 'not good enough' thoughts that might be phrased in terms of not being smart enough, successful enough, interesting enough, qualified enough, tall enough, popular enough, rich enough, young enough and so on.

'Not good enough' thinking becomes all the more damaging when another limiting framework called 'generalising' comes into play. As Brene Brown says in her great book, *Daring Greatly*, 'not good enough' is the language of shame that leaves us feeling as if there's something terribly wrong with us. You'll know you've lapsed into generalising if you find yourself taking the idea that you're 'not good enough' and turning it into 'never being good enough,' or 'not being good at anything.' The way out of this trap involves catching yourself whenever you notice you've been caught up in it, and deliberately rewriting the script. You can do this with a strategy that is very similar to the one I shared earlier when I talked about moving from a fixed mindset to a growth mindset.

Here's how it goes:

<u>Step One</u>
Recognise any negative or perfectionistic self-talk when it arises.

<u>Step Two</u>
Refute it with a corresponding positive statement.

<u>Step Three</u>
Take the kind of action a confident, self-assured person would take.

<u>Step Four</u>
Repeat Steps 1 to 3 as often as required.

PROCRASTINATION

Procrastination is another more or less evergreen mindset issue. I really don't blame you if you're questioning why procrastination sits under the banner of 'excuses,' rather than having a whole chapter of its own. The point I'm making by positioning it here is that it will only be a problem if you let it stop you from getting things done. The important words in the sentence I just wrote are 'if you let it.' In other words, a tendency towards procrastination does not exonerate you from taking responsibility for making sure you don't let anything stop you from doing the things you need to do to get to where you want to be. I may be wrong, but I'm pretty sure every book ever written was written by someone who had to deal with procrastination to one extent or other.

While I was writing my last book, *Mindset for Authors*, and reflecting on the question of the conditions that make it possible to overcome procrastination, I stumbled on Tim Urban's book, *Wait But Why*. Urban breaks the whole question down by identifying two types of procrastination. What differentiates these is how much is at stake. When there is nothing at stake, procrastination is an unbounded phenomenon that sits immovably between people and their goals. I experienced this kind of procrastination when I first got the idea of writing *Thrive in Midlife* back in 2009. Sure enough, writing a book was a no-brainer for someone like me. I say that because I wanted to use it to pave my way out of the stifling workday grind by establishing myself as a coach in a field I was passionate about. But even though it was a no-brainer, I still stuffed around for years, investing in every shiny object and other form of distraction I could lay my hands on.

The problem in 2009 was that I was comfortably ensconced in a job that provided me with a healthy six-figure salary. So there was really no urgency for me to write a book at that time. To put this in the language that Urban uses, there was essentially nothing at stake back in 2009, and there continued to be nothing at stake right up until the end of 2014.

As you'll recall from the timeline I shared with you earlier, everything changed for me when I was made redundant at the end of 2014. I bring this up again here because my redundancy took me from a place of not really having any skin in the game when it came to writing a book, to literally having my family's livelihood at stake. Among other things, this gave me a chance to see exactly what it feels like to deal with the second kind of procrastination. That's the kind we have a fighting chance against. In my own case, it was the desperation embedded in my circumstances that limited procrastination's ability to play fast and loose with me like it had during the previous five years.

One of the best ways for you to dampen the effects of procrastination is to sit down and write out a list of what's at stake for you. And if you think there is nothing at stake, I want you to revisit this question when you've read Chapter 6 on the hero's journey. And I want you to reflect on the fact you've had a calling to serve, even if you might not have thought about it like that before. So it's either a case of using your energy to go with it and answer the call, or it's a case of using your energy to resist it.

What I'm getting at here is that the calling never goes away. Even so, there are people out there who will resist it forever. This feels like a terrible shame to me. In fact, my life's purpose is to do whatever I can to help as many people as possible to avoid that fate. That's why I'm not pussy-footing around the issues here. It's not my job to be nice. It's my job to get you over the line so you can enjoy the benefits of being successful. And if your cage needs to be rattled for that to happen, then I'll be there to rattle it. My presence might take the form of a coaching arrangement if you chose to fast-track your journey to success by having me on your team, or it might take the form of the words in this book.

What I need you to understand right now is that you can't afford to be passive about this anymore. You have to be prepared to do whatever it takes to turn your mindset around. To that end, on the next page you'll find a space to list out what's at stake for you, and to answer some other questions that I've developed to help you to take a snapshot of how you are positioned mindset-wise right now.

NB: Please don't skip over exercises like 'The Mindset Snapshot' on the next page. I suspect you'll want to, but it's important that you do these exercises so that you can identify some of the baggage that has the potential to hold you back.

MINDSET SNAPSHOT

This exercise will allow you to take a snapshot of your current mindset. To prepare for this, I want you to sit comfortably and take a couple of nice long, deep breaths. Notice any tension in your body. Then notice what happens to that tension as you ask yourself the following questions:

What does success look like to me?
_____
_____

What's at stake when it comes to the success of my business?
_____
_____

On a scale of 1 to 10, how motivated am I to get to that level of success?
_____
_____

Am I applying perfectionism in any areas of my life?
_____
_____

How do I feel about those areas of my life right now?
_____
_____

In what ways am I doing really well in those areas of my life right now?
_____
_____

In which other areas of my life am I you doing really well?
_____
_____

What drains my energy?
_____
_____

What could I do to limit this drainage?
_____
_____

How easy or hard have I made it to feel good about myself?
_____
_____

What could I do to make it easier to feel good about myself?
_____
_____

Is blame, justification, denial, perfectionism, or any other thought process stopping me from doing the things I know I should be doing to build my business?
_____
_____

What has being stopped or slowed down by thought processes like the ones on the previous page cost me so far?
_____
_____

What strategies will I put in place to avoid being stopped or slowed down by thought processes like the ones I identified above?
_____
_____

Now consider what your answers to these questions mean in relation to your business goals, and write down any strategies you intend to follow through with to shift your perspective to a place of heightened self-belief where you are able to take consistent positive action towards your goals.
_____
_____
_____
_____
_____
_____
_____
_____

CHAPTER 4: DEVELOPING A SUCCESS MINDSET

Success is not an action, it is a way of life.
Brian Tracy

The first thing you need to do if you want to be successful is to be very clear about what success means to you. Is it about being able to send your kids to great schools, or have wonderful holidays, or live near the beach, or set up a charity around a problem you're passionate about solving? What I'm getting at here is that there's no point in buying into anyone else's idea of success. The internal fire it will take to sustain you can only be ignited by making sure your values and desires are being met while you serve the people who need the service you are offering.

Getting this piece of the puzzle right is about having absolute clarity, setting measurable goals, and putting strategies in place to ensure you remain accountable for taking the actions you need to take to achieve them.

It almost goes without saying, but I'm going to say it anyway. The best goal setting in the world isn't going to get you anywhere if you

CHAPTER 4: DEVELOPING A SUCCESS MINDSET

don't take action to implement your plan. What's more, success is anything but assured if your plan doesn't have a mechanism built into it to measure your progress and adjust your strategy whenever it needs adjusting. This isn't rocket science. It's actually pretty simple. In saying that, I'm not suggesting it's necessarily easy. The simple part is that after you've hooked into what you're passionate about, and set up some goals around that, you simply need to list the actions required to achieve them. The not so simple part is that for anything to happen, you need to take consistent strategic action on the things you listed. The reason this is not so easy goes right to the heart of this book, because without maintaining constant vigilance against mindset-related problems like procrastination, self-doubt and shiny object syndrome, there's a real risk that the actions you listed are not going to get done.

Underneath the basic principles mentioned above is the fact that your success is hinged on your ability to make calculated decisions. And mindset is terribly important when it comes to maintaining a psychological and emotional state that enables you to make decisions that are not clouded by things like people pleasing tendencies or Impostor Syndrome.

Having a positive attitude is also important. Operating from a growth mindset is key here because it will allow you to interpret any setbacks you experience along the way as learning opportunities. This is in stark contrast to the less positive interpretations people with a fixed mindset are likely to apply. These people tend to use words like 'failure,' 'stupid' and 'hopeless' at the drop of a hat. This question of attitude matters from a couple of perspectives. On the one hand, people like doing business with those they know, like and trust. And given that you can't convincingly fake positivity indefinitely, it's important to do the inner work to keep negativity at bay. I say this because it's just way too hard to like somebody whose demeanour brings us down. And on the other hand, there's the matter of maintaining energy. Without a doubt, negativity is a massive energy drainer, both for the beholder and for the innocent bystander.

You're allowed to be human of course, and as humans we're entitled to experience the full range of emotions. Maintaining a positive state is not about repressing negative emotions. It's about processing all of our emotions so we don't waste precious energy on trying to repress the things we don't want to feel.

GOAL SETTING

It's amazing how many people flap around in a vague space of wishing and dreaming for 'success' without building a foundation for positive outcomes to emerge. The way the mind works means that if there is no clear end point that has texture and shape to it, both your conscious and subconscious mind will be more or less powerless to help you get there. So what I want you to do now is clearly identify what you want. Then as long as you keep yourself accountable for doing the work, you will change your life forever by tapping into the abundance of opportunities that are out there, regardless of the existence of Covid or any other form of VUCA.

The key turning points in my life from the point of view of transitioning from a survival mindset to a success mindset were these:
- I got to see that I was responsible for everything that goes on in my life.
- I recognised I'd been playing small for most of my life because I took whatever was dished out to me, rather than deciding what I wanted and then setting out to get it with 100 per cent of my effort, and 100 per cent belief in my ability to do it.

- I learnt about the difference between fixed and growth mindsets, and realised I had to transition from a fixed to a growth mindset as fast as I possibly could.

I'm going to ask you to take a moment to see how you feel about where you are positioned visa-vis the kind of transition points I mentioned above. And regardless of what might have come out of that moment of reflection, I want you to do what a very dear friend urged me to do when I got to the point of having nothing to lose. I want you to do some blue sky dreaming. I'm suggesting this because a success mindset doesn't work on the lowest common denominator. It works on the plane of abundance. So when you sit down to set some goals, it's important that you don't allow them to be limited by what you've been able to achieve in the past. The exercise you did around beliefs earlier was aimed at enabling you to transition from a mindset built around scarcity, to one built around abundance.

What I'm inviting you to do here is create clear, vivid, exciting, emotional pictures of your goals, as if they are already exist. This is an incredibly powerful way to program your subconscious mind to do whatever it takes to bring your goals to life. It's very important to write these things down because for goals to be effective, they must be in writing. They also need to be clear, specific, detailed, measurable and time specific. In other words, it's critical to set a deadline or deadlines if you have sub-goals within your bigger goals. Your subconscious mind uses deadlines as 'forcing systems' to drive you towards your goals. Anticipating any barriers you are likely to encounter will enable you to be ready with any information, assistance or training you need to get to where you want to be.

BASIC GOAL SETTING EXERCISE

The question I want to ask you now is how would things be panning out in the following areas if nothing was in your way?

1. INCOME – how much money would you be earning this year, next year and five years from now?
   _____
   _____
   _____
   _____

2. LIFESTYLE – what kind of lifestyle would you have created for yourself and your family?
   _____
   _____
   _____
   _____

3. HEALTH – how would your health be different?
   _____
   _____
   _____
   _____

The following two supplementary questions are very important.

1. What is likely to get in your way and stop you from achieving your goals in these three areas of your life?
   _____
   _____

2. What are you prepared to do to make sure that nothing stops you from achieving your goals?
   _____
   _____

If any red flags went up for you when you answered these questions, I'd like you to contact me at jane@writewithjane.com to talk this through.

CHAPTER 5: THE MIND/BODY INTERFACE

The body achieves what the mind believes.
Bob Greene

There is a fundamental problem in a world like ours that is evolving at lightning speed and needs people who can come up with creative solutions to complex problems. The problem is that most of us respond to these circumstances by trying to outrun reality. The strategy we use to do this is to stay as busy as we possibly can.

This is absolutely the wrong way to go because this way of living limits our ability to respond constructively to challenging conditions. The paradox is that some folk wear their frantic lifestyle as a badge of honour. It's as if it means they are more important than everyone else because their crazy workload (and the stress that comes along with it) is proof that they are making a bigger contribution to the world than their calmer counterparts. On the contrary, living in a perpetual state of stress usually comes with the side-effect of keeping us stuck in overwhelm, confusion, hopelessness and any number of other non-productive states.

CHAPTER 5: THE MIND/BODY INTERFACE

Getting real with myself in 2014 when I was out of work for the first time in my life, enabled me to see that I was on a fast-track to nowhere with the amped-up stressed-out state I was in most of the time. In hindsight, I can see that if I didn't develop the ability to stay grounded and get a grip on my out-of-control stress levels, I was never going to get over the barriers I faced when it came to establishing a successful business.

One of the things I realised when I was working on my first book was that I had been using my ability to stay ridiculously busy to numb my emotions. It was only when I got good at pausing and relaxing that I was able to work out what I needed to do to get the book I'd started to write in 2009 finished. This awareness was also the key to my ability to leverage published author status to get lucrative speaking opportunities and more high-quality free publicity than I ever could have imagined.

Living a life where chronic stress is constant is a problem for business owners for two reasons. On the one hand, it drains our energy, and on the other hand it takes us out of the part of our brain that is conducive to organising our thoughts and expressing them in a coherent and meaningful way. That's because stress can only exist when the body's sympathetic nervous system is activated. We are operating from the most prehistoric part of our brain called the limbic system when the sympathetic nervous system is on. The limbic system only has one job to do. That job is to make sure we survive. In other words, it couldn't care less if we hit our aspirational goals or not.

It's the prefrontal cortex we need to be operating from to function effectively. Among other things it gives us access to our creativity and our ability to organise our thoughts so that we can produce meaningful content to connect with our audience. We also need an active prefrontal cortex to access our capacity for self-discipline. This is why I give my clients tools like my tailored *Creativity Priming Meditation* to help them manage their stress. I developed this powerful tool with the help of a kinesiologist and performance expert called Anikiko. Anikiko's backing tracks have been used to improve results in a wide range of environments, from healing retreats to Fortune 500 companies. I feel blessed to have been able to incorporate her years of experience into the tool I developed to give my clients the edge when it comes to getting into a state that is conducive to both creativity and productivity.

As you will have gathered by now, I take the business of creating a fertile internal environment very seriously. That's because everything changed for me when I connected the dots between the fact that we live in a crazy stressed-out world, and the fact that less than 20 per cent of the people who start businesses actually manage to sustain a 'reasonable' lifestyle.

Of course, not everyone who is busy is stressed. But no matter what your actual circumstances are, staying connected to your body's innate ability to relax is going to make it much easier for you to take the action you need to take to keep moving towards your goals.

What you need to know is that it's just as counterproductive to try to do anything that requires executive decision-making skills when we're tired, as it is to try to do these things when we are stressed. As Kelly McGonigal says in her book, *The Willpower Instinct*, "Even being mildly but chronically sleep deprived makes us more susceptible to stress, cravings, and temptation of all kinds."

Finding out about the link between things like willpower, brainpower, stress and sleep is often a defining moment for the people I work with. Some have been struggling to get important projects like writing a book finished for years or even decades, because among other things, their body's limbic system is running the show most of the time. Finding this out is a bit of a double-edged sword really. I say that because on the one hand, it's a relief for my clients to realise that it's their body's survival instincts and not a character flaw that is rendering them helpless in the face of distractions. Meanwhile on the other hand, a heightened level of accountability comes with the knowledge that what they need to do to turn things around is take responsibility for the outcomes they achieve.

If you're someone who has trouble getting a good night's sleep, I want you to know you are not alone. Almost 2,000,000 people, or a little less than 10 per cent of the entire population in Australia where I'm based, share this problem with you. I'm going to give you hope by filling you in on what I found out when I sought professional help for my less than ideal relationship with sleep.

The first thing you need to do to get a good night's sleep is to lower the amount of adrenaline in your body. Adrenaline is one of the stress hormones that triggers the fight or flight response. The ideal package of lifestyle choices that will help you to maintain healthy levels of adrenaline include:
- exercising regularly
- maintaining a high level of nutrition and hydration
- taking responsibility for managing your life in a way that minimises the amount of stressful events you're exposed to on a day-to-day basis
- relaxing by whatever means work for you.

NB: You'll find exercises at the end of this chapter that will help you with the last point.

For my part, I had to go right back to basics when I learnt about the extent to which stress and sleep deprivation were compromising my ability to get my first book finished. This mattered because I was relying on the content and the leveraging opportunities presented by the book to start my business and build my profile. What's more, I needed to start generating enough money to replace the six-figure income I lost when I was made redundant as soon as I possibly could.

Back in the day, I wasn't only addicted to being busy, I was also addicted to overthinking in general, and worrying in particular. The way out of this destructive pattern was to learn how to get out of my head and into my body.

Believe me, this was far from easy at first. In fact, I fought against it as if my life depended on hanging on to the crazy schedule I'd lived with for years. Fortunately, I eventually started to get the knack of slowing down. I did this by adopting the daily practices you'll find at the end of this chapter. I also got strict about minimising the distractions I allowed into my life in general, and especially the places I slept in and worked in. This included making some very simple but incredibly effective changes, like turning off the notifications on my phone. I now live happily without that annoying noise that signals the arrival of an email or text message. I also limited myself to only opening emails and text messages twice a day. I won't go on about the other practical ways I went about creating the conditions for my prefrontal cortex to stay engaged most of the time, except to say that there are some wonderful books available on time management and efficiency that you might like to investigate if you decide you want to make the conditions you live under less chaotic.

Basically, I want you to do whatever it takes to create the conditions you need to get your business set up and running efficiently. There isn't a 'one size fits all' remedy I can offer you here, except to say there will be things you need to cut out of your life, and there will be things you need to put in. One of the things I definitely want you to think about is the fact that you can calm yourself down almost immediately by becoming conscious of your breath. So whenever you notice that you are purposely avoiding working towards your goals, or getting a bit wound up for whatever reason, I want you to deliberately take a number of long deep breaths to get out of the state you're in, before you fall headlong into a full-blown stress attack.

This might feel a bit awkward at first, especially if you've never thought about the way you breathe before. But in the spirit of a growth mindset, I want you to relax in the knowledge you'll get better at this the more you practise. It's both ironic and completely understandable that the idea of focusing on our breathing and getting back into our body doesn't feel natural at first, especially if we've been pumped up on adrenaline for most of our life. It's actually the most natural thing in the world. But as we move through the years, we seem to overlay so many 'stories' on top of who we really are. That's why coming back home to our core can feel like a huge journey. In one sense it is a huge journey. In fact, it's a hero's journey for some people, even though all we need to do to re-embody and ground ourselves is to go back to the fundamentals of breathing and pausing. That's all it takes to bring a gentle but profound transformation about.

What mindfully pausing throughout the day does for us on a physical level is dial down our sympathetic nervous system. As you now know, the sympathetic nervous system is not concerned about long term goals. Therefore, it has no part to play in making it easy for us to stick to our plans to commit time to the projects we are working on at any given time. This is because we need to have our parasympathetic nervous system switched on to access the willpower we need to keep ourselves on track.

Another problem with having our sympathetic nervous system running the show is that it makes it almost impossible to access our higher order cognitive skills. These include things like the ability to organise our words in a way that will communicate our thoughts clearly enough for other people to understand them. Dialling down the sympathetic nervous system enables us to re-engage our parasympathetic nervous system so we can calm down and think more clearly. It's only in this state that we're able to be compelled by the reason we set time aside to work on our goals. That's because willpower is at its best when we unconsciously weigh up the consequences of not doing 'the harder thing.' We need to be able to do that, because as the procrastination expert Tim Urban says, we all prefer to do what's easy and fun. Needless to say, it's not the parts of our business we find easy and fun that we're likely to be procrastinating over. That said, one of the great benefits of being successful is that we can delegate the parts of our business we don't find easy and fun to others. But if your business is not at that level yet, you'll be needing access to your prefrontal cortex now more than ever.

I'm covering the question of stress in as much detail as I am here, not only because access to our prefrontal cortex is critical to our ability to get past the hundred and one distractions we're likely to encounter in the average day, but also because we need our prefrontal cortex to be activated to get past any resistance to being visible and/or successful that we might be harbouring. It doesn't matter whether the resistance relates to Impostor Syndrome or something else altogether. The bottom line is that resistance results in even more stress, and the more stress we experience, the less likely we are to be able to make progress towards our goals.

CHAPTER 5: THE MIND/BODY INTERFACE

Living with chronic stress is like swimming in a rip in the ocean. We're culturally programmed to value action, but action in a rip equates to struggle, and the struggle will wear us out eventually. On the other hand, if we dive under all the activity by breathing deeply and coming back into the present moment, we'll reach a point where we can be still, and our body's calm response can kick in. That's the place where our capacity for creativity and productivity is most readily accessed.

Suzanne Segerstrom from the University of Kentucky describes the body's natural ability to relax as a kind of pause and plan response. This is not as well known as the idea of the fight or flight response, but it is equally important. What I'm suggesting here is that you plan to pause regularly throughout the day. I've included some daily rituals at the end of this chapter for you to embed into your routine to help you get really good at calming down. This is important because getting your stress under control will not only make it much easier for you to operate at a high level of efficiency and effectiveness, it will also result in better health and everything else that being at your best will open you up to.

What I want you to experience through doing the 'Mind Decluttering Exercise' and the 'Four Daily Rituals' on the following pages, is how much more relaxed and clearheaded you'll feel once you empty out some of the clutter that's in your mind. You probably have no idea how much of an energy drainer you're harbouring with the unconscious material you've got rattling around in there at the moment. But believe me, you will definitely notice the difference when the load is lessened.

MIND DECLUTTERING EXERCISE

The aim of this exercise is to get everything out of your head and on to the page. Whether it's about booking yourself in to see your dentist, or calling a friend you haven't seen for a while, or getting your tax done. Whether it's a nagging concern about getting fat or dying young, or whatever it is. Get it all down on paper.

You might be surprised to see what's been lurking in the back of your mind for God knows how long.

You start this exercise by writing down everything that's on your mind at the moment. Give yourself as long as you need, and when you think you've finished, ask yourself "What else?"

Once you've got your master list ready, I want you to turn to the next page with the heading, *Things I can do something about*. Then write down all of the things on your master list that you can do something about. Again, when you think you've finished, I want you to ask yourself "What else?"

Then go to the page with the heading *Things I can't do anything about*, and write all of those things down. And again, when you think you're finished, ask yourself "What else?" The idea is to get it all out of your head and on to the page.

Once you've finished that list, I want you to schedule into your diary any key actions that need to be taken to resolve the things that you can do something about.

There's no disputing the fact that sometimes life gets in the way and stops us from getting everything we schedule into our diaries done by the date we'd planned. While a reasonable level of justified slippage is not an issue, it's important to notice tasks that seem to be getting rescheduled indefinitely. Identifying these things enables us to look into whether there is any emotional baggage or unrealistic expectations attached to these tasks. Being able to see this playing out may well enable you recognising any tendencies toward self-sabotage that you might not have been conscious of before.

Last but not least, you need to fold the page of with the list of things you can't do anything about in half, so the edge of the page is folded into the middle. It's not uncommon for my clients want to do something dramatic like ripping the page out and burning it, flushing it down the toilet, or something like that. I'm not of a mind to treat the page like that, because just because something is on this list of things you can't do anything about doesn't mean that it's not important. It just means you don't need to have it occupying the valuable real estate in your head all of the time.

To my mind, it's worth doing this exercise at least three times a year to gauge how everything is going.

To summarise, what you need to do here is:

1. List out everything that's on your mind. We call this **List A**.
2. Copy everything on **List A** that you can do something about onto **List B**.
3. Copy everything on **List A** that you can't do anything about onto **List C**.
4. Schedule everything that's on **List B** into your diary.

WHAT'S ON MY MIND
List A

THINGS I CAN DO SOMETHING ABOUT
List B

THINGS I CAN'T DO ANYTHING ABOUT
List C

FOUR DAILY RITUALS

These rituals are designed to help you remain positive, focused and energised.

It calls for an investment of about three minutes, three times a day.

One of these rituals is done first thing in the morning. One is done in the middle of the day. One is done before you go to bed. And the last one is all about honing your awareness around negative thoughts and feelings that emerge during the course of the day. And using this awareness to transform the energy around these thoughts and feelings so that they don't get in your way.

These are deceptively simple yet very powerful exercises that I urge you to add to your routine. If you practise these rituals regularly, you will slowly but surely change your state and take your life to a whole other level.

Don't be critical of yourself if you don't get around to doing all of the rituals every day. Even doing just one of them from time to time will improve your state. So imagine how much difference it could make if you got into the habit of doing these exercises as they have been written.

THREE GROUNDING MINUTES
To be done every morning on waking.

1. Take a moment to remember what you're grateful for. Sit quietly and just feel this gratitude in your body for two or three minutes. Simply notice any thoughts that cross your mind without engaging with them at all. Don't be distracted by the idea that you need to do anything about these thoughts.
2. Then think about what you plan to achieve today, and embed the idea of what you need to do to achieve this in your mind and your body, as well as writing down the actions you need to take on one or more Post-it notes that you can stick wherever you'll be able to see them during the day. The fridge usually works for me.
3. And lastly, make a point of reviewing the progress you are making towards your daily goals at least twice a day.
4.

You should definitely consider booking a session with me at www.writewithjane.com if you struggled with this, or if your daily goals continue to be missed. Together, we'll tease out what's going on for you, and disrupt any patterns that could otherwise cost you dearly in terms of the time it takes to get your business to where you want it to be.

THREE FOCUSED MINUTES
To be done somewhere around the middle of the day.

1. Sit quietly with your eyes closed and just notice all of the parts of your body working beautifully. If there's only one place in your body that feels good on a particular day, concentrate on that part.
2. During this time, soundlessly say to yourself: "I have everything I need to run a successful business." Or anything else that needs to be said, like perhaps "I am enough," or "I am happy, healthy and strong," or "I'm infinitely abundant." Whatever it is, repeat this mantra in your head very slowly and firmly for three minutes.
3. Notice if you're holding on to any tension in your body. Just breathe into that place and notice the breath enveloping the tension until it dissipates.
4. After three or so minutes, bring your attention back into the room by wriggling your toes and stretching your arms above your head. If there is any unresolved tension in your body, ask yourself what needs to happen for this tension to be released. Sit with this question until an answer comes up, or until the tension dissipates.
5. If nothing changes after a little while, ask yourself: "Am I prepared to let this tension go now?" If nothing comes up for you, just ask: "What needs to happen for me to be ready to let this go?"
6. Repeat this question until you get an answer, or the tension dissolves, or until you feel like it's time to stop. Your body will continue to process the material that comes up during this exercise overnight. It might take more than one day for some things to clear, but the cumulative effect of daily focus should ultimately release the tension.

THREE RELAXING MINUTES
To be done every night before you go to bed.

1. Sit comfortably with a pad and pen nearby. Close your eyes, breathe deeply and just relax into your body. Notice any thoughts, feelings, emotions, worries, sounds, smells or other sensations that arise. Don't engage with them. Don't try to suppress or change them in any way. Just observe them.
2. Maintain this practice for three minutes. Then open your eyes and notice your body supported in the chair. Notice what you can see, smell and hear. Wriggle your toes and stretch your arms above your head to ground yourself in the here and now.
3. Now write down your responses to the following questions.

   What ideas or feelings came up during the exercise?
   _____
   _____
   _____

   What is at least one thing you like about yourself?
   _____
   _____
   _____

   What is at least one thing you did well today?
   _____
   _____
   _____

   What is at least one thing you feel grateful for?
   _____
   _____
   _____

DAYLONG MINDFULNESS

To be done whenever you notice negative thoughts coming up.

Notice any negative thoughts that come up throughout the day. Notice how and where you feel these in your body, and ask yourself the following questions.

Where did this thought come from?
_____
_____
_____

What need, issue or problem does this thought serve?
_____
_____
_____

What can I do to address that need?
_____
_____
_____

How does this thought limit me?
_____
_____
_____

What would a more resourceful thought be?
_____
_____
_____

Now take a few moments to consider the way the resourceful thought has made you feel.

CHAPTER 6: THE HERO'S JOURNEY

We do not have to become heroes overnight. Just a step at a time, meeting each thing that comes, seeing it as not as dreadful as it appears, discovering that we have the strength to stare it down.
Eleanor Roosevelt

You're in for something really special if you're not familiar with the hero's journey. It's likely to completely change the way you think about your place in the world, and the way you relate to any challenges you face from this point forward.

What I want you to do right now is stop reading and press play on the video you'll find at www.writewithjane.com/about/. This video explains the hero's journey through the perspective of *The Hunger Games*. If *The Hunger Games* isn't your cup of tea, there are several other videos on YouTube that are equally valuable. I especially like a couple that look at the hero's journey through movies like *The Wizard of Oz*, *Harry Potter*, and *Star Wars*. So head over to YouTube using 'the hero's journey' as your search term, and see what you find that resonates with you.

I'll always love the hero's journey because if I hadn't stumbled on it when I did, there is no way I would have been able to finish my first book. Not to mention being able to go on to write and speak in a number of different forums where I'm seen as an expert when it comes to helping people to step into their story and find their inner hero. But perhaps the biggest journey of all for me has been in developing a business mindset. To put that statement into context, I want to remind you that I spent my whole working life through to middle age employed in the bureaucratic bubble of the Australian government. I wasn't there for no reason. I was there because it was an excellent environment for me to play small.

It seems like a lifetime ago when my journey to becoming a published author began. It was in 2009 when I took a sabbatical to get formal qualifications in coaching. Looking back on it now, it's clear that the universe was pointing me towards my life's purpose when I bumped into the long lost friend I told you about earlier. What I didn't mention earlier was that this happened two days after I finished the coaching course I was doing. That chance meeting led to the experience that convinced me I should write a book to build my coaching practice around. At the time, I was working as a senior manager in one of Australia's largest museums while trying to grow my small coaching practice on the side. I was ever so slowly getting myself ready to ease my way out of the comfortable employment I had outgrown many years before redundancy made push come to shove at the end of 2014.

Meanwhile, I decided to buy an online program that gave me templates and tutorials on book-writing that helped me get me off the starting blocks. But before too long I was derailed by a negative mindset that got louder and louder every time I tried to hunker down and write. I found myself more or less powerless against the voice in my head that told me that no one would want to read a book written by me because I wasn't an expert, I wasn't qualified enough, I wasn't a good writer, and I wasn't even an interesting person.

The part of this self-inflicted negativity that really knocked me off course was the part about not being qualified enough. So I wound up doing another coaching course. Rather than begrudging the time and money involved in doing that, I'm actually grateful for the digression because the course I chose to do introduced me to the hero's journey.

As you will have seen in the YouTube video, the framework of the hero's journey came out of Joseph Campbell's fascination with mythology. Joseph Campbell was an American academic and author whose book, *The Hero of a Thousand Faces*, popularised the idea of the monomyth. You've seen how this plays out in the video, and I'm going to add another opportunity for you to get your head around this wonderful formula for telling stories by describing the way it plays out in Harper Lee's much-loved book, *To Kill a Mockingbird*.

Atticus Finch is the hero in *To Kill a Mockingbird*. He is the archetypal father figure. His call to adventure is delivered when he's given responsibility for defending an African American man who is accused of rape. This results in a deep internal struggle for Atticus because he knows defending the accused man, Tom Robinson, is the right thing to do. But because of the racist milieu of the Deep South in the 1930s where the drama is taking place, he also that knows that if he takes the case on his family will be exposed to intimidation or worse.

The moment when Atticus decides to accept the case represents his point of departure from the ordinary world. This is a place he will only return to once he moves through the dark and very uncomfortable territory the journey entails. The idea of crossing a threshold is key to the hero's journey framework. Atticus is in no doubt he has crossed a threshold once the trial begins, because things come to a head with his children being attacked by Bob Ewell. This is the way payback for taking the case on manifests in *To Kill a Mockingbird*. In the end, Ewell is killed by the simpleton Boo Radley, who plays out his own hero's journey when he overcomes problems with agoraphobia to step up and save the children.

The children being attacked by Ewell represents Atticus's crisis point at 6 o'clock. This is when his worst fears about the consequences of doing the right thing by defending Tom Robinson come to pass. This is classic hero's journey material. The hero always faces their darkest hour before emerging back into the ordinary world in a totally transformed state.

My own darkest hour came when I realised the home my family had lived in for over twenty-three years would have to be sold because I had lost my job, and the comfortable income that came along with it. I will never forget the deep sense of despair and desperation I felt at that time, especially in light of the fact that in spite of spending over $30,000 and five years of my life on the project of becoming a published author, I still didn't have a book to establish my authority and credibility as a coach. The kicker for me was that along with experiencing a raft of negative emotions resulting from being made redundant, I was also experiencing a sense of shame and guilt in relation to spending such a big chunk of my family's money on a project that had been so spectacularly unsuccessful.

All of this added up to an immense sense of vulnerability for me. Fortunately, my awareness of the hero's journey kept me from defaulting to behaviours and thinking that had essentially kept me small for my whole life. I can only speculate on how low I might have gone if I hadn't stumbled on the coaching course that introduced me to the hero's journey. But I can confidently say that things wouldn't have ended up nearly as well for me as they have.

The fact that a reward of some kind always follows the crisis point is central to the hero's journey framework. In *To Kill a Mockingbird*, the reward for Atticus comes in the form of the children being saved. In my own case, I was rewarded by being able to work out what had prevented me from getting my book written for so long. This enabled me to finally get it done, and to build a business around helping other people do the same thing.

I decided to focus my coaching business on book-writing because of the transformation I experienced in the process of becoming a published author. That experience was nothing short of cathartic. And through it, I realised that what I was put on this earth to do is help other people to experience the incredible power of stepping into their story by writing a book, and leveraging published author status to get access to the myriad of opportunities like free publicity and high profile speaking engagements.

The hero's journey was particularly helpful when it came to teasing out exactly what had held me back as I was writing *Thrive in Midlife*. You might remember from the introduction that the first time I faltered was when I gave up on my book in 2010 because my fixed mindset was telling me I was not qualified enough to be a successful coach. In hindsight, I can see that this manifestation of self-doubt was a blessing in disguise. That's because even though it held me up terribly in terms getting my book finished, it also caused me to do more training, and that training introduced me to the hero's journey.

Among other things, the hero's journey framework enabled me to see that I had it in me to overcome any barriers I encountered along the way to becoming an author. What's more, it showed me that it was fine, and in fact it was even necessary for me to seek out help whenever I needed it. I was able to recognise that the darkest part of the journey was all about my reluctance to step into the spotlight because of my crippling shyness, which wasn't helped by my parents coaching me as a child to not be a show pony or big-note myself.

This background effectively primed me to get good at playing small. Working on my self-belief turned out to be one of the more important things I did in the process of writing *Thrive in Midlife*. Essentially it enabled me to develop the mindset I needed to get to where I am now. In fact, it's clear to me now that it wasn't only the Halo Effect at play when I started attracting more people into my coaching business off the back of my first book. In hindsight, I can see that this result was equally attributable to the kind of person I'd become through overcoming the barriers around owning my story, and being prepared to be seen for who I really was.

HERO'S JOURNEY EXERCISE

So with all of this in mind, I want you to put yourself centrestage and consider the following questions:

How do you feel about stepping into the role of a successful businessperson?
_____
_____

Can you see your desire to establish a business as a call to adventure?
_____
_____

Have you answered the call yet, or is it still sitting on your bucket list?
_____
_____

What caused you to answer the call? (If you haven't answered the call yet, move on to the next question.)
_____
_____

What is holding you back?
_____
_____

What will it cost you if you fail to answer the call?
_____
_____

What specific obstacles are you likely to encounter along the way?
_____
_____

What resources will you tap into to overcome those obstacles?
_____
_____

Who will you call on when you need help?
_____
_____

On a scale of 1 to 10, how confident are you about getting your business up and running successfully over the next twelve months?*
_____
_____

On a scale of 1 to 10, how important is it for you to achieve this?
_____
_____

Regardless of how you answered the question above, when you think about returning to the ordinary world as a successful businessperson, consider these questions:

How will you be feeling?
_____
_____

What will be different about you?
_____
_____

What will your life look like?
_____
_____

What opportunities will you be taking advantage of?
_____
_____

* If you rated the likelihood of getting your business up and running successfully over the next twelve months below an 8, I urge you to book in for a complimentary chat with me at www.writewithjane.com. If I can't help you directly, I have some wonderful experts on my team who I'm pretty sure will be able to get you on track.

CHAPTER 7: THE AUTHOR'S JOURNEY

*It's all right to have butterflies in your stomach.
Just get them to fly in formation.*
Rob Gilbert

It can be challenging for my clients to develop the degree of self-belief they need to be able to make the possibility of becoming an author, and building a successful business around their book, actually happen. That's why they often wait for months or even years before they get around to connecting with me.

At the most fundamental level, my clients get to borrow my belief in them while they cultivate their own. The part of the process I love most is when I see people transform the doubt they are feeling into a bourgeoning belief in the idea that it's actually possible for them to write a book that will position them as an expert.

For example Joel Annesley, whose story you will read in a moment, attended one of my introductory workshops back in 2018. He had a wonderful story to tell but he was stifled by crippling self-doubt. Despite this, he made a commitment. That commitment started his journey towards published author status. His commitment was that no matter what life threw at him, he would see his book through to completion this time. My commitment to him was that I would have his back 100 per cent of the time. I became his mentor, his cheer leader, his sounding board and his butt-kicker.

What started as an idea that couldn't quite be articulated when we first met, soon transformed into something truly inspirational. I'm incredibly proud to have witnessed not only the birth of Joel's book *Quiet Confidence: Breaking Up With Shyness*, but also the exponential growth of the wonderful business he developed off the back of his book.

I feel truly blessed to be able to include Joel's reflections on his hero's journey for you here.

AN AUTHOR'S JOURNEY: JOEL ANNESLEY

I preface my contribution to Jane's book with the notion that writing your own book isn't for the faint hearted, and neither is building a business. It was somewhat uncanny just how the act of writing, and the process of turning my book into reality and a business, sheepishly followed the hero's journey. I don't by any means consider this a negative. Actually, there was something deeply comforting about it. When you know what the hero's journey looks like, you learn to go with the flow.

I can always recall the desire to share my story about how I overcame my shy and anxious identity. I'd picture what it would be like to have my words in print for the world to see. My only problem was that I had a belief that it wasn't possible. My brain sent me messages that I must be an illiterate fool, and it would only result in humiliation should anyone glance at my words on paper. There was an inner conflict, a war that grew within. A creative genius that wished to flourish fighting an authoritarian who gave the order of silence. I was frozen, too terrified of what the world might think of me.

Stuck in my ordinary world, I saw the call to adventure come and go time and time again. I refused the call and the years passed. I had the goal of writing the book, but it was a mere pipe dream. I didn't believe it was actually possible. It wasn't until I met Jane Turner that this changed.

Within a few hours, I had accepted the call to adventure, met my mentor and crossed the threshold into an exciting new world. I had made the commitment.

The writing process itself, albeit very personal, is something of a collaborative effort; I could not have made it to the finish line without a mentor and allies. I left each 'Power Writing Weekend' that Jane runs with renewed focus and vigour to push through to the next boundary. There were many challenges along the way, and I developed a love-hate relationship with my writing. Some words I cherished, some I absolutely loathed. Some moments I thought about dragging it all to the recycle bin. But I continued on the path. Whenever I felt challenged and self-doubt raised its ugly head, Jane gave me the encouragement I needed to restore faith and belief in myself.

I saw the hero's journey unfold in front of me. I was on the journey and I sensed my darkest hour was near. It was about the three-quarter mark where finishing my book felt so close, yet still so far.

The problem was – I hated my book. It's a strong word, but it's the truth. I reflected on the many hours I'd invested in the process, only to see the formation of half-baked ideas. The inner perfectionist had raised its ugly head. It was my darkest hour where I questioned the point of my work, the book and everything really.

But there was someone who never did. Someone believed from day one that I would make it to the finish line. She saw me through the darkest hour, and she wasn't fazed one bit. She gave me strength and confidence to continue, to push myself and defy the odds. That someone was Jane Turner. With her help the barriers had finally fallen, and the words were flowing.

I'm pleased to announce I finished my book. In the final hours, my heart was racing and the adrenaline was pumping right up until the very last sentence. The journey was finally over. I reflected on the journey, noting just how far I had come. I had crafted the art of the written word and I couldn't be more grateful. This has served me well in business because as they say, 'content is king' and the words we use matter when it comes to getting our message out there.

Before I started the journey, my book was just an idea. When I was standing behind the podium launching it, I was challenged to hold back the tears. I recall times as that young anxious child who would visualise his future-self telling him it would all be okay. It was as if, in that single moment, I was looking at that young, confused boy and sharing the words he only dreamt of hearing – "You, just as you are, are enough."

I tell you this story because the entire journey up to the launch of my book was one I will always cherish. I can't wait for you to go through that journey for yourself if you are thinking of writing a book. If you've already been there, and your focus is now on building a business beyond your book, I want to share some of the priceless lessons I've learned since embarking on the journey of establishing my own business.

Being part of Jane's 'Power Writing Program' not only gave me the passion and confidence to want to continue writing, but it also gave me confidence to turn my book into a business where I could help others overcome anxiety and shyness.

Once you become a published author, your life changes. While I won't sugar coat my experience and say it's been all roses since, I can certainly say that Jane couldn't be more correct about the existence of the 'Halo Effect.'

Following the launch of my book, I've had the opportunity to be featured on podcasts and local radio, and I've stepped onto the stage at Jane's Author Showcase events. What's more, my words have been quoted on social media, and even quoted on reputable media sources such as *inc.com*.

I share this with you because I want you know that if I can do it, so can you. I'm not interested in counting how many times I've been featured here or there. The things I value most are the personal messages sent to me from people who have been touched by the book. I also love the uncanny stories about how they stumbled across the book in the first place. That is a real testament to the power of putting your words into print.

I wrote my book with a modest goal. That goal was based on the value of even just helping one person, and if that one person was me, then so be it. I enjoyed the book-writing journey and embraced the idea that the outcome didn't matter. It healed me, and then I ventured on to build a coaching business. Writing a book is an incredibly focused creative process that I consider to be a wonderfully passionate art form. Building a business, on the other hand, entails wearing many hats and an almost infinite number of decisions and choices about how you might structure and market your services.

Quite frankly, my initial experience beyond the book was a bit of a low. I called this phase a moment of 'post-task depression,' where the journey was now over, and I found myself in overwhelm about what was to come next. I had completed one 'hero's journey' and found myself smack bang at the beginning of another. Stepping into the business world felt like jumping out of the comfortable pond into the great blue ocean – endless in terms of both opportunities and decisions.

If I could highlight the biggest takeaway for me so far, it would be to **let go of unrealistic expectations of yourself.** In the development of your business, the darkest hour exists in the realms of overwhelm. I'd been running the program of 'too much to do, too little time' in my head for far too long. I had tried to wear too many hats to the point that I couldn't keep them all on my head at once.

Business success can't occur with an impatient mind and a body that can't keep up. There's no point falling over the finish line in a heap of exhaustion. When you reflect on the book-writing journey being more valuable than the outcome itself, you realise this applies to all parts of life. With that perspective, business success exists in the beauty of balance. A healthy balance between productive time, and the necessary downtime. In the mindfulness classes I now run, I speak of the balance between states of 'doing' versus the state of simply 'being.' It's incredible how much 'doing' can be achieved after experiencing the simple state of 'being.'

While I am still incredibly passionate about my mission and my unfolding journey, I've dropped the unrealistic expectations I once placed on myself. I give myself permission to get the right balance of sleep and rest, along with precious time to 'live.' While it's taken a long time to get to this point, I'm incredibly happy with where I am right now. I'm playing the business game at my own pace. This reminds me of a quote by Bill Gates:

> *Most people overestimate what they can do in one year and underestimate what they can do in ten years.*

That initial sense of overwhelm came from the lack of a clear process coupled with goal posts that were unrealistic. But something quite magical happens once you have that 'aha' moment where you get to see that the majority of problems we face are just dusty old programs we've been running over and over again. You realise your past cannot be your future if you choose to run programs that support you and guide you towards becoming the best version of yourself in your business and in your life.

You don't need to compare yourself to others and you can choose to no longer give yourself unrealistic expectations. This race only has one participant, and that's you. If you run too fast, you'll miss out on the beauty that is the journey. You can be you, and you can do it your way.

As I embark on my own next chapter, I'm about to emerge on the other side of becoming a qualified Clinical Hypnotherapist and Strategic Psychotherapist, where I'm blessed to add more tools to my toolbelt to help my clients tackle their lifelong battles with anxiety with ease.

As I reflect back on this incredible journey, I can't thank Jane Turner enough for her coaching and mentorship. As I like to say, **"It all started with a book."** I was delighted when Jane gave me the opportunity to design a *Success Mindset Meditation* for you. I hope you enjoy it and go on to thrive in your business.

CHAPTER 8: CHOICE

I am not a product of my circumstances.
I am a product of my decisions.
Stephen Covey

The word 'choice' might seem benign enough to you now, but believe me, it's actually the most powerful word in this book. It's the word that puts you wholly and solely in the driver's seat when it comes to building a successful business. We make hundreds of decisions every day. Some aren't particularly consequential. Deciding to have cereal for breakfast rather than toast is not going to be life changing. But the decision we unconsciously make about how successful we are going to allow ourselves to be certainly is.

As I said in the introduction, working with an unsupportive mindset is one of the biggest barriers first time businesspeople are likely to experience. Awareness of the importance of mindset enabled me to finally finish my first book, and to develop the *Power Writing Program* that I now share with coaches, consultants, businesspeople and entrepreneurs all over the world.

The thing for you to think about now is whether you are going to do whatever it takes to overcome the barriers you encounter in the process of following your life's purpose. This question sounds simple enough I know, but sadly this is where it all comes undone for many people. That's a real shame, because all that sits between people and their goals is whether they are going to choose to back themselves and do the work involved. That might be the 'inner' work that this book is focused on, or it might be the 'outer' work of building their profile, setting up systems and services that address the needs of their potential customers, and following a strategic approach to communicating their message in a way that is heartfelt and congruent.

What I want you to understand is that no matter how many times you've been hijacked by a less than resourceful mindset in the past, what matters now is whether you are going to choose to go for growth and continue to progress towards your goals, or whether you're going to choose to stick with familiarity, and settle into a false sense of comfort and security.

While I totally respect your right to choose, I need you to know that continuing to resist the call to establish your business, and/or take it to the level it should be operating at, means you are never going to feel fully satisfied because you won't be able to achieve the level of success you rightly deserve. So before you finish this book, I have one more exercise for you to do to bring together what you've learnt so far.

The first thing I want you to do is go to www.writewithjane.com and download the *Success Mindset Meditation* that Joel Annesley put together for you. This will help you to fine-tune your mindset and get on with the job of establishing your business without any white noise that would otherwise get in the way. After you've listened to the meditation, I want you to close your eyes and imagine how you will feel when you're living the life having a successful business will enable you to live. Allow yourself to feel the feelings that come up when you think about this. Then make a short 60-second video talking about your business on your phone.

I'm gifting the meditation to you because I want the video you make to be a powerful tool for you to regularly look back on for clarity and motivation, especially if things like uncertainty and doubt start to creep back in at any stage.

On a cautionary note, I want you to know that it will do you no good at all to just sit on the material I'm sharing with you in this book. Without taking action, you will not only fail to move closer to your business goals, you'll also essentially be putting another nail in the coffin of hope. That hope will invariably get weaker and weaker as you load additional delays and disappointment on top of the half-hearted attempts you've probably already made.

I see this happen way too often, and I've fallen prey to it myself many times. In fact, as I said before, I was only able to get out of the incredibly unproductive cycle that wound up costing me $30,000 and five years of my life in the process of writing my first book, because I was able to substantially shift my mindset. So please don't procrastinate on this and tell yourself you'll do the exercises in this book later. Both you and I know you probably won't. It's time for you to put your past behind you and move forward by breaking the old patterns that no longer serve you. So, make that video and use it as a tool to prove to yourself that you are no longer a person who wants to build a successful business. You are a person who is actually doing it.

My heartfelt wish is that you will enjoy abundant success and satisfaction around the legacy you build. I'm not saying it will always be easy, but I am saying it's eminently doable, especially if you tap into the resources I've made available for you at the end of this book.

CONCLUSION

I've run the race you're running in terms of answering the call to build a business you are passionate about. And I have the scar tissue to prove that I resisted doing the mindset-related work involved for way too long. Believe me, I know every trick in the book when it comes to papering over the cracks and unconsciously prolonging the process of getting to the level of success we deserve.

My mission in life is to help people like you to step into their power and spread their message. It's important that mindset interference doesn't get in the way because there are plenty of savvy attention getters out there who are ready to overshadow you.

I want to wish you all the very best from the bottom of my heart. If you haven't already done so, I want you to download the *Success Mindset Meditation* that Joel Annesley has created to help people like us to realise our dreams.

All you need to do now is take a look at the areas of expertise my panel of experts cover. You'll find this in the appendix section that follows.

Here's to your success,

Jane Turner

REFERENCES

Daring Greatly: How the Courage to be Vulnerable Transforms the Way We Live, Love Parent and Lead, Brown, Brene. (2013) London. Penguin Books.

Mindset: The New Psychology of Success, Dweck, Carol. (2012). London. Little, Brown Book Group.

Risky is the New Safe, Gage, Randy. (2012). Audible Inc.

The 7 Habits of Highly Effective People: Infographics Edition, Covey, Stephen R. (2015). Mango Publishing Group.

The Brain That Changes Itself: Stories of Personal Triumph from the Frontiers of Brain Science, Doidge, Norman. (2008). USA. Viking Penguin. A Member of the Penguin Group (USA) Inc.

The Hero of a Thousand Faces (Third Edition with Revisions), Campbell, Joseph (2008). New World Library.

The Power of Now: A Guide to Spiritual Enlightenment, Tolle, Eckhart (2011). Hachette Australia.

The Willpower Instinct, McGonigal, Kelly. (2012). New York. Avery. A Member of the Penguin Group (USA) Inc.

To Kill a Mockingbird, Lee, Harper (2002). Harper Perennial Modern Classics.

Wait But Why Year One: We finally figured out how to put a blog onto an e-reader (Kindle Edition), Urban Tim (2013).

Why Zebras Don't Get Ulcers, Sapolsky, Robert M. (2004). New York. McMillan Publishers.

REFERENCES

ONLINE SOURCES

What makes a hero? - Matthew Winkler,
https://www.youtube.com/watch?v=d1Zxt28ff-E&t=4s

Inside the mind of a master procrastinator? - Tim Urban,
https://www.youtube.com/watch?v=arj7oStGLkU

Anikiko - https://www.music-nutrition.com

Joel Annesley - www.joelannesley.com

RESOURCES

These are the trusted experts that I refer my clients to.

For advice on financial management - Amanda Fisher:

Amanda is a Financial Educator who helps business owners to unscramble their numbers to improve cash flow and profits. Amanda says that "building a business to achieve your goals requires not only an understanding of the numbers, but what to look out for and how to use financial reports to make informed decisions that will impact the financial results of your business."

You can tap into the resources that Amanda has made available at https://www.thecashflowqueen.com/

For advice on sales - Sharon Grant:

Sharon left the corporate world because everyone told her she'd be a 'Natural Born Salesperson.' After many failures and trials, she discovered a method that enabled her to sell elegantly in a way that felt natural. With thousands of hours helping hundreds of entrepreneurs make millions of dollars, she shares her *Elegant Sales Success* strategies with those who want to be able to tap into their natural ability to sell elegantly.

You can access the resources that Sharon has made available at https://elegantsalessuccess.com.au/

RESOURCES

For advice on communication skills in general, and difficult conversations in particular - Tim Higgs:

Tim is an expert on Leadership and Communication. He helps leaders, managers and business owners to develop the skills and the presence needed to deliver excellent results. He simplifies topics such as Influence, Difficult Conversations and EQ so that they are easy to master.

Tim is also the best-selling author of *Emotional Judo: Communication Skills to Handle Difficult Conversations and Boost Emotional Intelligence.*

You can access the resources Tim has made available for you at https://emotionaljudo.com/

For advice on business in general - Adriana Cecere:

Adrianna runs programs to help businesspeople get more of the right stuff done faster. She helps her clients to gain clarity and direction with an action plan, and accountability strategies to achieve their goals.

You can access the resources that Adriana has made available at https://www.consultingaustralia.com.au/

ABOUT THE AUTHOR

Jane Turner is the author of four books including the bestselling *Mindset for Authors: How to Overcome Perfectionism, Procrastination and Self-doubt*. She is also an international speaker and sought-after Book Writing Coach.

As well as holding Master Coaching qualifications through the Behavioral Coaching Institute, Jane is also an NLP Master Practitioner with a gift for seeing a solid book structure come out the targeted questions she asks her authors-to-be.

Jane is the person behind the ***Power Writing Program***, the ***Power Publicity and Promotion Program***, the ***Power Writers Publishing Group,*** and the ***Author Business Hub***. She works with people all over the world from her base in Sydney Australia where she lives with her husband and teenage daughter.

Visit www.writewithjane.com to see the range of programs on offer.

You can follow Jane at:
https://www.facebook.com/writewithjane/
www.writewithjane.com

www.ingramcontent.com/pod-product-compliance
Lightning Source LLC
Chambersburg PA
CBHW020327010526
44107CB00054B/2008